PRINT CASEBOOKS 8

The Best in Environmental Graphics

Written by
Akiko Busch

Published by
**RC Publications, Inc.
Bethesda, MD**

Introduction

First published 1989 in the United States of America by **RC Publications, Inc.** **6400 Goldsboro Road** **Bethesda, MD 20817**

Manufactured in Hong Kong
First Printing 1989

PRINT CASEBOOKS 8/THE BEST IN ENVIRONMENTAL GRAPHICS (1989-90 EDITION)
Library of Congress Catalog Card Number 75-649585
ISBN 0-915734-59-1

PRINT CASEBOOKS 8 (1989-90 EDITION)
Complete 6-Volume Set
ISBN 0-915734-56-7
3-Volume Set No. 1 ISBN 0-915734-63-X
3-Volume Set No. 2 ISBN 0-915734-64-8

RC PUBLICATIONS
President and Publisher: Howard Cadel
Vice President and Editor: Martin Fox
Creative Director: Andrew P. Kner
Managing Editor: Teresa Reese
Art Director: Linda Decker
Associate Editor: Tom Goss
Editorial Assistant: Susan Scarfe

The judging panel reviewing this year's *Casebook* submissions for environmental graphics was the first to admit that its job is not an exact science. To begin with, the category itself can be difficult to define, since it is often an adjunct of architecture, landscape, interior, or lighting design, to name only some of the variables. Indeed, the graphic designer's role can be difficult to pinpoint. While jurors made an effort throughout their review of entries to analyze how signing programs worked within the parameters established by those other variables, or to ascertain how well programs had been assembled around them, it was frequently difficult to know exactly what the role of the graphic designer was. All too often, presentations were unclear on this point, and jurors appealed to future entrants to clarify the scope of their work.

Too, criteria inevitably shift from project to project, and establishing what they are to be can be a vague, nebulous process in itself. Nevertheless, this year's panel looked for originality and innovation, in both concept and execution, as testimonies to design excellence. Time and again, jurors were overheard saying, "I haven't seen that done before"; or, "That's a new application of material." The Citicorp Bicentennial Flag was perhaps the single most startling image in terms of sheer innovation. At the same time, however, high-performance graphics, though not particularly innovative, were prized for their purely straightforward sense of function—witness the U.S.

Army Corps of Engineers Sign Standards Program.

Graphics programs were also evaluated in terms of how accurately they reflected their contexts. Was the program designed for a zoo? A shopping mall? A luxury hotel? An industrial park? Was it appropriate to its site?

Tied into this, often, was the question of regional interest. There is, thankfully, a growing trend for environmental graphics to visually note the particulars of their surroundings. Many retail shopping malls, for example, now reflect a concerted effort to refer to local folk art and cultural history, and their designers make it a point to highlight the details that might differentiate a mall in New Orleans from one in Topeka. Indeed, such details have a sense of integrity, even honesty, about them, always welcome in such manufactured environments. (Why is it that a shopping mall is invariably dubbed a "galleria," a "village," or a "pavilion" by its developers —anything, that is, but the shopping center it really is?) Jurors applauded efforts such as these. Likewise, signing programs by Sussman/Prejza were cited for their proud flaunting of a Southern California sensibility.

The innovative use of standard, even generic, materials distinguished a number of other selected entries. Signing constructed of chain-link fencing for an industrial park won instant approval as a low-cost solution that was nevertheless appropriate, functional, elegant. Too, jurors observed the

increasing use of natural materials—metals, stone, terra cotta. "For a few years, it looked as though we were limited to plexiglass and acrylic," noted one juror with noticeable relief. In some cases, the use of such natural materials was connected to a local or regional look, as mentioned above, its use determined by those materials indigenous to the area. In other cases, it was an effort to appear solid, simple, homespun, "under-designed." In almost all cases, it was welcomed.

Similarly, the jurors noted limited creative use of photography. The mega-photos used in the construction fence for H. Stern Jewelers made a glowing exception, and prompted jurors to suggest that future entries include more evidence of commonplace processes like photography, as well as commonplace materials. Indeed, in an age when environmental graphics are so often distinguished by the extravagant use of lavish materials, due credit was given to the imagination, restraint, and wit demonstrated in programs using more basic materials in more creative ways, like, for example, the rock, pottery and forged steel employed in the Cottages at Coffeepot signing.

These qualities, then, are what the jurors looked for in making their selections. But what did the multitude of entries *not* selected suggest? As in previous *Casebook* judgings, the jurors commented on persistent problems in typography, finding that, all too often, legibility suffered for the sake of style. Overly elegant

scripts, poor positioning of type and inappropriate point size often disqualified programs that were otherwise well-conceived.

Jurors also expressed surprise that greater advances hadn't been made with electronic signage. While programs such as that for the Garden State Park Racetrack confidently integrated electronic graphics into a broader system, jurors had hoped to see many more instances of such imaging in less obvious sites, such as museums. "That would be real innovation," noted one.

A number of programs also begged the question of being over-designed, contributing to a sense of visual overload. Although there was praise for the tastefully sculptural sheaf of wheat at the Owings Mills Mall, some jurors found that the sculptural signing increasingly found at retail shopping malls was "almost too much." Self-serving, the sculptures often tend to establish themselves as independent design elements rather than as elements that have been practically and functionally integrated into their environments. (Do such visually excessive graphics and sculpture detract attention from storefronts, rather than direct attention to them, as had been their original purpose to do? Juror Ann Dudrow, who has developed a number of signing programs for such malls, defended the approach, commenting that "this is the MTV approach. People in these environments *enjoy* being barraged by such imagery." The question found no conclusive answers in the jurors' ongoing discourse, and it promises to be asked again in an

age when such aggressive visuals, in everything from packaging to corporate identity programs to signing, seem to have become the norm.

Too, there were entire areas of environmental graphics noted by jurors for competence, function, elegance, but faulted by them for a lack of innovation. A number of programs for service stations had been submitted, and the jurors invariably commended them. All the same, their uniformity prevented their selection. "I haven't seen anything *new* in this area of street furniture and signing since Mobil first broke the mold in 1965," observed one panel member.

Perhaps it was the need for relief during the rigorous task of reviewing so many entries in such a short period of time, but the panel was invariably amused and enlivened by programs that demonstrated their own sense of wit and humor. Almost any episodes of true visual humor were greeted with appreciation and pleasure—witness the unanimous enthusiasm awarded the H. Stern construction fence, the Orange Outdoor Advertising fake billboards, and the Vignelli oversize construction-barricade blueprints. All of these sparked the imagination of jurors.

Programs such as these should not, however, be dismissed as frivolous incidents of comic relief. Rather, by taking neither themselves nor the purposes they serve too seriously, by engaging the imagination, and by suggesting a lightness of spirit, they make certain inroads in the excess of more ponderous graphics that saturate the environment.

The tedium of judging so many entries in one day and the effort to judge each program afresh amidst a visual barrage is, after all, not so different from the visual assaults that greet most of us each day, particularly those of us who live and work in the urban environment. Visual overload is the norm, and a day of judging *Casebook* entries is really nothing more than a microcosm of the input we all receive, the perceptions we have, the judgments we inevitably make daily. Let graphic designers take special note, then, that there is always a place for episodes of visual humor and wit in the *Casebook* submissions, and, more to the point, in the environment at large. *—Akiko Busch*

Mark Barensfeld   **Thomas W. Casey**   **Ann L. Dudrow**   **Michael D. Reed**

Mark Barensfeld is a founding principal of Schenker Probst Barensfeld in Cincinnati, a firm specializing in print graphics and environmental and exhibit design. He has taught design at Ohio University, Art Academy of Cincinnati, and the University of Cincinnati. Established in 1980, his firm has acted as consultant for Cincinnati's Bicentennial design standards guide; in developing signage programs for a multi-purpose park and four-and-a-half mile historic district along the Ohio River; and in developing signage and graphics for a 500,000-square-foot, multi-purpose museum. The firm's work in graphics and exhibition design for zoological, historical, and natural history institutions has won awards for excellence and has been the subject of articles in various publications.

A graduate of Ohio State University School of Architecture, Tom Casey has worked with the firms of Page, Arbitrio & Resen and Paul Arthur, as well as the architectural firms of Hardy Holzman Pfeiffer in New York City, Brooks Barr Graeber & White in Austin, Texas, and Skidmore Owings & Merrill in Chicago. He is currently a partner of Greenboam & Casey Associates, Inc., New York City. Established in 1979, the firm specializes in environmental graphics, corporate graphics, and exhibition design for clients that have included Edward Larrabee Barnes Architects, the Carlyle Hotel, Sheraton Hotels, Metropolitan Life Insurance Company, and numerous other architectural firms, cultural institutions, and investment property owners. Casey's work has been published in Architectural Record, Better Buildings, Japan Architect, PRINT, and Progressive Architecture. He was 1988/89 president of the Society of Environmental Graphic Designers.

Now an associate principal at RTKL in Baltimore, Ann Dudrow is a graduate of Rhode Island School of Design. She has worked extensively in logo design, promotional graphics, sign-system design, and architectural graphics for corporate, hotel and retail projects. Her varied professional background includes work with, successively, the Rouse Company in Columbia, Maryland; Brown & Craig, Inc., in Baltimore; Langston-Tasi Associates in Columbia; and Tetrad, Inc., in Annapolis. Her project experience has included architectural graphics for clients such as Union Trust Tower in Baltimore, USF&G Corporate Training Facility in Baltimore, St. Louis Centre in St. Louis, and numerous retail malls and plazas. Honored by awards from the Art Directors Club of Washington, DC, and the Society for Marketing Professional Services, her work has been published in *Print Casebooks* and PRINT's Regional Design Annual.

A graduate of Ohio State University, Michael D. Reed in 1973 founded Mayer/Reed in Portland, Oregon, a multi-disciplinary product, interior, and graphic design firm. The firm's work consists mostly of large-scale design commissions for architectural and landscape environments, with a client roster that includes the Portland Center for Performing Arts, the Oregon Convention Center, the Arizona Historical Society Museum, and Vancouver's Expo '86. Reed is a member of the Board of Trustees for the Oregon School of Design and serves on the Board of Visitors for FIDER (Foundation for Interior Design Education Research). Serving as chairman of the Graphics Committee for the National Board of Trustees for IBD (Institute of Business Designers), he reorganized the group's corporate identity programming.

Casebook Writer

Akiko Busch

Index

Projects

Akiko Busch is a writer and editor in design, architecture, and crafts. Her books include *Wallworks* and *Floorworks*, published by Bantam Books; *The Photography of Architecture*, published by Van Nostrand Reinhold Co.; and *Product Design*, published by PBC International. She also served as guest editor for Industrial Design magazine's 1983 and 1984 annual Design Review issues. She has written numerous articles appearing in Metropolis, American Craft, Industrial Design, How, PRINT, and other design publications.

Clients/Sponsoring Organizations

Designers/Architects Consultants

Citicorp Center
Bicentennial Flag
in Lights

The idea of using a building to illustrate a message may not be new. Sign painters over the years have known that the peculiar dimensions and height, not to mention locations, of specific buildings can make them ideal places to paint, plaster, and otherwise display oversize messages. It is more difficult and unusual, however, to actually incorporate the existing architecture of the building as part of the design, and more unusual still to use light as the medium. Yet Ronné Bonder did both of these things in creating a memorable, albeit fleeting, moment of graphic drama—Citicorp's immense flag honoring the Bicentennial of the U.S. Constitution.

Bonder had originally planned to suspend vertical strips of fabric from the sides of the building on New York City's East Side, but the aerodynamics of updrafts rendered the plan impractical. On closer scrutiny of the building, however, Bonder found that the steel facade between the windows of each floor "created perfectly spaced *horizontal* white stripes." By simply filling in the rows of windows with red and blue, he could create a huge image of the flag. Each flag on the four sides of the building measured 180′ wide and 70′ high.

It was not, of course, a question of "simply filling in the windows." Bonder had chosen the 53rd through 59th floors—the uppermost and therefore most visible levels of the building—to be the "site" for the flag. That made for 21 windows of red and 13 windows of blue per side on the 56th though 59th floors, with 34 windows of red per side on the remaining floors. A whopping 30,000 square feet of red and blue plastic was subsequently ordered in 56 pre-cut 70″-by-22″ panels for corner windows and 896 70″-by-54″ panels for side windows.

Getting the 30,000 square feet of plastic fabricated and cut within four weeks proved the greatest logistical feat. That done, however, beginning at 5 p.m. on the evenings the flag was to be displayed, a team of 100 porters, electricians, security and management staff all worked to install the panels and the interior lighting which was to tap into the building's central electrical system. And at 8:30 on the evenings of September 16 and 17, 1987, honoring the 200th anniversary of the U.S. Constitution, and again on the weekend of July 4, 1988, from 9 p.m. to 2 a.m., switches were pulled and the flag unfolded, stripe by stripe. Or as it were, floor by floor.

As the sixth tallest building in Manhattan and with a landmark sloping roof, the Citicorp building is an indisputable urban beacon. By exploiting the site in such a way, and by recognizing its innate sense of theater, Bonder created a superbly dramatic moment memorable to all its witnesses. In the onslaught of graphics honoring the Bicentennial in less memorable ways, this surely was a grand achievement.

Client: Citicorp Corporate Marketing Div., New York City
Design firm: Ronné Bonder Advertising Ltd., New York City
Fabricator: Ain Plastics, Inc.

1.

3.

1, 4. The program included a T-shirt with the logotype image of the illuminated building as well as a press-kit folder, poster, and letterhead.
2. The only drawing (on back of business envelope) ever made for the project delineates line-up of panels while attached lucite chips identify colors. Designer Ronné Bonder says the Citicorp building and the roof of the building where his own office is located became his "sketch pad." Working from his roof by mobile phone with a team at Citicorp, he was able to test various reds (2) and blues (4) as to distance from light source and depth of hue in order to reach the proper American flag colors.
3. Poster includes an image of the building against fireworks.
5. The Citicorp Bicentennial "flag" occupies windows of the 53rd through 59th floor windows.

2.

4.

5.

The Cottages
at Coffeepot

The striking red-rock landscape, clear skies, and the landmark Coffeepot Mountain itself make up the site for The Cottages at Coffeepot, a 37-home development in Sedona, Arizona. Understandably, then, in designing the logo and signs for the development, the designers looked to the spectacle of the surrounding landscape for directives. The objective, they explain, was to devise a signing program comprised of "natural" materials that would complement the natural environment— sandblasted rock, sandstone etching, forged steel, forged iron castings, copper, brass, and various woods, as well as earthtone colors such as light gray, rust, and terra cotta.

Working within a design budget of $5000, the designers first did a photographic audit of the location. Along with rough sketches, it established the tone for the program that in the end included, besides logo and signs, environmental graphics applications, sales literature, print advertising, letterhead, and a public-relations kit.

The logo itself is comprised of a tree representing "shelter and the commitment to preserve the natural environment"; a profile of Coffeepot Mountain; and the image of the sun symbolizing the favorable climate. Their stylized rendering permits applications on elements "as small as a postage stamp and as large as the site entrance signing." More to the point, the logo suggests the same spirit of enviromental compatability that the development highlights. The hand-rendered main logotype along with Americana

1.

Uncommon Homes in an Uncommon Setting

Uncommon Homes in an Uncommon Setting

the Cottages at Coffeepot

Uncommon Homes in an Uncommon Setting

1. Exterior signing takes its rough-hewn cues from the natural landscape.
2-5. Earth-tone colors and organic materials are used in a variety of signing.
6-8. Logo and logotype were developed as a stylized rendition of elements in the surrounding landscape.

type for body copy continues the naturalistic flavor of the program. Completed within a six-week design schedule, the program reflects both its geographic surroundings and the development of homes it represents.

The *Casebook* jurors cited the integrity of the overall program, remarking particularly on the use of indigenous materials. "It's almost naive," said one. "Not over-designed," said another. While it should perhaps go without saying that any graphics program that classifies itself "environmental graphics" might be sensitive to its environment, programs such as this are the happy exception rather than the rule.

9.

9. *Promotional material includes a folder, letterhead, and poster.*
10. *Table settings include a welcome card.*

10.

Client: Phil W. Morris Co., Sedona, AZ
Design firm: Robert Brookson Design, Inc., Phoenix
Designers: Robert Brookson, Mary Nord
Consultant: Norm Kitzmiller, Kitzmiller Marketing Group, sales and marketing
Fabricator: Phil W. Morris Construction Co.

Garden State
Park Racetrack

"Horseracing faces an aging and declining audience," the designers of Garden State Park Racetrack explain. "The challenge for racetracks is to attract new patrons by making their facilities exciting entertainment—a 'fun' alternative to casinos, shows, or restaurants. At Garden State Park, signs were designed to uncomplicate the site and its buildings. Signs were also used to educate, inform, and entertain visitors in a way that was new to racetracks." With these objectives in mind, the designers developed a program that stressed consistency without monotony.

The vast mixed-use site of the 285-acre Garden State Park Racetrack in Cherry Hill, New Jersey, demanded a diverse signing program for a 500,000-square-foot grandstand building; a sales pavilion that accommodates auctions as well as betting; and an area known as the backstretch where all support systems for the track are housed. This last includes 27 stables, five dormitories, administrative buildings, barns, paddocks, and a recreational building; and the corporation yard for maintenance facilities, a car wash, print shop, and garage. The total of 49 buildings ranges from small to enormous, old to new, public to private, while users include one-time visitors along with seasonal residents, trainers, and track employees. How then to develop a consistent signing program that might meet such a diverse set of needs?

A combined use of Franklin Gothic and Caslon 540 Italic typography, accent shapes, and color maintain visual continuity

1.

2.

1. New logotype is in Franklin Gothic.
2. A sign used at the old racetrack projects an outdated image.
3. Illuminated letters inset into the canopy were used for the Clubhouse entrance signing.
4. Interior illuminated lettering marks the Grandstand entrance.
5. Fiberglass pylons signal the racetrack's vehicular entrances.

3.

4.

5.

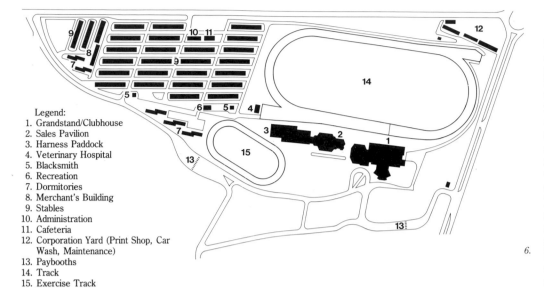

Legend:
1. Grandstand/Clubhouse
2. Sales Pavilion
3. Harness Paddock
4. Veterinary Hospital
5. Blacksmith
6. Recreation
7. Dormitories
8. Merchant's Building
9. Stables
10. Administration
11. Cafeteria
12. Corporation Yard (Print Shop, Car Wash, Maintenance)
13. Paybooths
14. Track
15. Exercise Track

throughout the program. Aluminum, plexiglass, brass, plastic laminate, neon, fiberglass, and terrazzo were all used to construct non-illuminated, internally and externally illuminated, neon, and LED message signs, many of which are changeable or removable. Full-size mockups were constructed in many cases to determine the correct scale. Indeed, one of the things that consistently marks the success of this expansive program is the appropriate scale of all signing, be it small informational plaques or oversize numbering. Further specifications that were met by

6.

7.

8.

9.

6. *Site plan reveals the extensive scope of the signing program.*
7-8. *Neon signing distinguishes refreshment stands and restroom entrances.*
9. *Hexagonal accents illuminate betting windows.*
10. *An electronic message board welcomes visitors to betting windows.*

10.

the Philadelphia design firm of Cloud and Gehshan Associates called for:

● Lettering for the grandstand that included illuminated letters inset into the canopy and a neon medallion at the face of the canopy. For the colonnade, the designers coordinated with the architect to determine letterspacing of letters and metal panels. That the entire signing system represents a "racetrack of the future" is clear in the installation of an electronic message board, replacing the traditional chalkboard. Plugged into the racetrack's timing

system and infield toteboard, the message boards have both static and dynamic capabilities.

● An aluminum signing system for the backstretch, most notably oversize, 6' saw-cut numbers that identify all new stables. The *Casebook* jurors were especially lavish in their praise of these large directory numbers on the sides of the stables, finding their size and application "extremely visual and appropriate for such a large area."

● Directional and identification signs for the sales pavilion with a hexagonal accent at the top referring to

11.

12.

13.

14.

11. Signing for recreation buildings combines typefaces.
12, 13. Caslon 540 Italic has been used for dorm and stable signing.
14. Six-foot-high, saw-cut aluminum numbers identify new stables.

the shape of the building; and betting windows with similar illuminated accents.

Working within a sign fabrication budget of $1.25 million ($750,000 for signs; $500,000 for the electronic message boards), Cloud and Gehshan devised a graphic vocabulary for Garden State Park that indeed renews and revitalizes the image of the raceway. They dramatically exploited the sense of excitement and entertainment, the atmosphere of mystery, and at times even glamor that all factor into the classic image of horseracing, and transcribed these in an up-to-date, lively, contemporary language.

Client: International Thoroughbred Breeders, Cherry Hill, NJ
Design firm: Cloud and Gehshan Associates, Philadelphia
Designers: Virginia Gehshan, designer; Ann McDonald, co-designer for sales pavilion building
Architect: Ewing Cole Kraus
Fabricator: Letterama, Inc.

15. Floorplans and directories are positioned strategically throughout the Grandstand/Clubhouse building.
16. Signing for the Phoenix betting windows are illuminated white in a black field.
17. Half-inch-thick polished brass letters mark the Phoenix lobby.

15.

16.

17.

Hold Everything
Stores

The graphics program for Williams-Sonoma's Hold Everything stores—five stores in California, each one averaging 3500 square feet—focused on designing an organized visual marketing program for a line of products themselves meant to organize one's life. The products include shelving, containers, time-saving gadgets, and storage systems of all sorts and sizes for kitchen, bedroom, bath, laundry, and closet. And although they represent a broad product line, they are without any necessarily consistent design quality. The graphics, of course, were not meant simply to identify, market, and promote the goods, but to install a visual liveliness throughout the stores and to indirectly suggest the products organizational capacities.

The designers from Gensler & Associates in San Francisco relied upon the use of bright, cheery colors—PMS 285 Blue, PMS 185 Red, PMS 123 Yellow, and PMS 326 Green—and strong, simple

1.

2.

1. The entryway logo is a stylized rendition of a four-sided box.
2. Wall displays at the rear of the store demonstrate the function and use of assorted products.

shapes for the entire program, which included shopping bags, gift boxes and tags, merchandise tags, business cards, gift certificates, all exterior signing, product display systems, special product promotion panels, and other interior indentification. The logo is an abstract representation of a box, with each wall of the four-sided box rendered in one of four colors.

Working within a design budget of $25,000 and using metal, paint, wood and acrylic, the designers developed a system that visually organized the diverse product line. The central device was a series of three-dimensional boxes, painted in bright colors with a silkscreened text, used both to provide visual relief and to articulate the products' various functions. A wall system against the rear wall displaying an array of gadgets includes both written explanations and demonstrations of use. Bodoni Bold Condensed and Futura Medium were the typefaces selected as "simple, clean faces with character."

The *Casebook* jurors agreed that the program made for a cohesive package, at once visually engaging and accurately reflecting the overall efficiency of the product line.

Client: Williams-Sonoma, San Francisco
Design firm: Gensler Graphics Group/ Gensler & Associates Architects, San Francisco
Designers: John Bricker, design director; Barbara Leistico, designer
Fabricator: Pischoff Co.

3.

4.

3. Three-dimensional boxes with a silkscreened text elaborate on organizational devices for bedroom and closet.
4. Hexagonal sign system illustrates different shelving components.
5. The promotional program includes gift boxes, shopping bags, tags, and business cards.

5.

The Children's District of Central Park

When Frederick Law Olmsted and Calvert Vaux laid out the plan for New York City's Central Park in 1858, they designated the area south of 65th Street, then the city's most accessible and most visited area, the "Children's District." Today, that area includes the Dairy/Central Park Visitor Center, the Chess & Checkers House, the Hallett Nature Sanctuary, and the Belvedere Castle Learning Center.

The signing system designed for the Children's District by Mentyka/Schlott Design of New York City makes an effort both to collaborate with the existing landscape and architecture of the park and to reflect the 19th-century flavor of the district. The intent was to provide information about these different areas and to establish their various graphic identities, and the *Casebook* jurors agreed that the signing achieved both ends without being intrusive. There was no directional signing, for example. As the designers explain, "Just as the original designers desired, we would leave the public to enjoy their wanderings on the park path system, discovering wonderful views and structures without needing to be pulled out of the environment to digest information. Therefore, limited building identification near the sites, and signing which offers interesting information about their past and present function, was our general guideline."

It was a guideline well chosen. Neutral colors relating to historic buildings in the park were used. Vandal- and weather-resistant materials— photo-anodized aluminum in

1.

1. Dairy signing is photo-etched aluminum with a painted cedar wood frame.

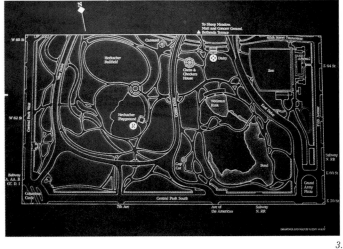

2.

3.

4.

5.

6.

2. A visitor examines the angled outdoor area map.
3. The district map highlights different areas and the path systems connecting them.
4. Signing for Hallett Nature Sanctuary offers information about wildlife.

5. A Victorian sensibility is suggested by the typeface used for the Dairy.
6. Plan of Dairy indicates placement of signing.
7. Sandwich board sign for Chess & Checkers house allows for posters and brochures to be replaced.

7.

8-10. The chiseled masonry work of the Chess & Checkers house (drawing) suggested the use of Albertus typeface, as shown in early studies. Final signing employed photo-etched aluminum with cedar frames.

8.

9.

10.

most cases—were selected for obvious reasons. The metal was "visually tempered" through the use of stained or painted red cedar frames, and specifications called for a dark ground and silvery type. This treatment downplayed the harsh, reflective qualities of metal which Mentyka/Schlott felt would be inappropriate to the site.

The designers used a variety of typefaces, each of which they felt correlated to the specific site: For the Dairy, ITC Isbell Medium, with its faintly Victorian frill; for the Chess & Checkers House, Albertus, which they found "masonry-inspired, or chiselled"; for Belvedere Castle, Folkwang, with a medieval flavor; and for the Hallett Nature Sanctuary, Bembo, which was consistent with the park's publications program.

Designers worked within a budget of $10,000 and a schedule of one year.

Typefaces were tested for legibility and full-size comps were constructed to determine the placement of key elements. Collaborating with the park's landscape architects and historians, the designers felt that they "came to better understand the landscape and the impact signing could have on it."

The jurors concurred unanimously. They were impressed in particular by the overall restraint of the graphics program and applauded the use, in many instances, of the gray frames. "This is subdued," observed one juror. "The designers haven't used bright colors, and the signing doesn't interfere with nature exhibits, as the primary color palette used in many exhibits for kids so often does."

Client: Central Park Conservancy in cooperation with City of New York Parks and Recreation Dept.
Design firm: Mentyka/Schlott Design, New York City
Illustrator: Glenn Wolff
Fabricators: R. H. Guest, Inc. (sign fabrication), Metalphoto of Cincinnati (photo-anodized sign faces)

Marine Industrial Park

Developed on the site of an old military base to accommodate industries that had been displaced by waterfront commercial development, Boston's 225-acre Marine Industrial Park has a diverse tenant roster: the Boston Design Center, Massport Cruise Terminal, fishing and shipbuilding industries, along with light-manufacturing concerns. Future renovation plans for the park include outdoor public art, waterfront parks, and other amenities. In designing an exterior signing program, it was the designers' intent not simply to establish site identity and to provide orientation information, but to "tie the site together and link the wide range of tenants and use."

While the graphic vocabulary of such industrial landscapes tends to be improvisational, adapting to time and to the changing needs of tenants, the designers in this case devised a language that could be adopted for everything from entrance signing to tenant guidelines. Explains Jon Roll of Jon Roll and Associates, "We decided to adopt a 'high industrial' look for all graphics—bold, colorful, and large-scale (the site could take it)." It was an industrial look rendered most notably by the use of chain-link fencing, the most commonly used material on the site. Entrance identification signs and drydock identification signs are constructed in chain-link letters, 8' high and mounted on existing fencing.

1.

2.

3.

4.

5.

1, 2. *Oversize lettering on generic chainlink fencing establishes the program's industrial look.*
3. *An aerial photo of the site reveals its scope.*
4, 5. *Four-foot by 10-foot aluminum slabs were used for major identification signs.*
6. *Secondary destinations are numbered with "flag signs."*

6.

25/Environmental Graphics

The solution presented considerable problems. Because mesh is essentially "loose," and will not by nature hold a shape, the designers and manufacturers worked out a technique to cut and finish the ends of the stretched chain-link fabric. As Roll notes, "The 'grain' of the chain link was altered for each letter stroke."

Large, brightly-colored aluminum slabs have been used for all other identification, and directional signs in the shape of arrows convey a clear message. High-gloss finishes have been applied to all signs. The typeface—Universe Bold Condensed Italic, selected for its forward, contemporary look—tends to be oversize, legible almost in the extreme.

Overall, the program is bold, utilitarian, even elegant, reflecting a brisk atmosphere of commerce and industry. The *Casebook* jurors applauded the application of generic chain-link, and found the entire program appropriate, upscale, and upbeat.

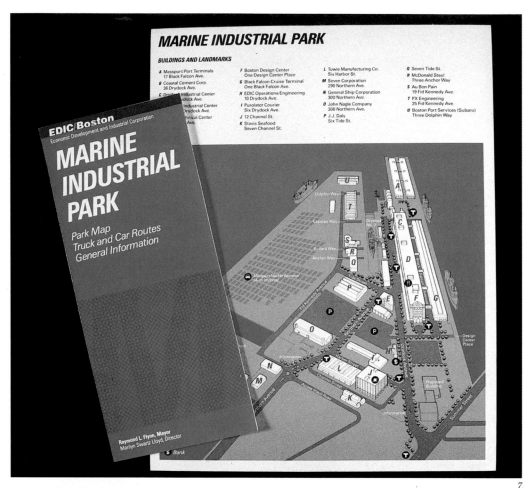

7.

7. Promotional material includes a map of the site indicating different tenants.
8. Directional signs are arrow-shaped.
9. An aluminum slab information board with a map of the site greets visitors.

8.

Client: Economic Development and Industrial Corp./Boston, Boston, MA
Design firm: Jon Roll and Associates, Cambridge, MA
Designers: Jon Roll, Sarah Speare, Whitney Perkins
Fabricators: Cornelius Architectural Products; Expert Fence Co.
Consultants: Carol Johnson Associates (landscape architects), Fay, Spofford and Thorndike (engineers)

9.

Summit Green Building

Located in an office park in Greensboro, North Carolina, the Summit Green Building is distinguished by its elegant linear form, anchored by three massive towers. Horizontal bands of gray concrete, exposed metalwork that has been painted white, and the use of three different kinds of glass make for a restrained, polished exterior. On the interior, granite floors, architectural glasswork and glazed white tile further that image.

The designers for the building's graphics—Jan Lorenc Design, Atlanta—speak of the symbiotic relationship achieved between signing, architecture, and landscaping; and of integrating the signing program with the philosophical underpinings of the architecture. "The opportunity to work directly with architects with a strongly-held and carefully articulated design philosophy has allowed for a level of meaning and a degree of effectiveness in our own work which is not available in every project," they state.

Indeed, the rewards of such a collaborative approach are evident throughout the signing program, which included the entrance sign at the building's exterior, a building identification sign, site directional signs, site regulatory signs, project regulatory signs, marketing signs, an interior directory, floor directives, and door signs. The porcelain-white aluminum plate specified for base material made for appropriate visual massing. A Bodoni typeface was used for its "modulation of thicks and thins that echo the crisp, classical forms of both signs and buildings." And the

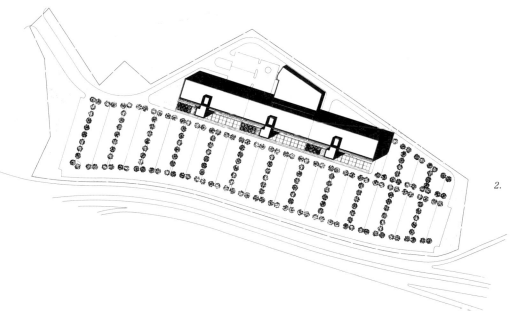

1.

2.

1. Sculptural exterior signing coincides with the sculpted facade of the building.
2. A site plan illustrates the linear, three-tower design of the building.

minimalist palette—gloss white with black and gray typography—reflected that of the building itself.

Accomplished within a design budget of $40,000 and a one-year schedule, the polished simplicity of the graphics reflects that of the site. The tight detailing, placement of type, materials, finishes, and deliberate positioning of the signing is consistent with the minimalist lines of the building.

"The building was designed to display fine joint details and the modulation of texture and grid. We developed the signing to be cognizant of these details, and to function as a design detail in itself," conclude the designers. The *Casebook* jurors agreed that they did exactly that.

Client: Cousins Properties, Inc./IBM Corp., Marietta, GA
Design firm: Jan Lorenc Design, Inc., Atlanta
Designers: Jan Lorenc, Jeffery L. Beilfuss
Architect: Gwathmey Siegel & Associates, New York City
Fabricator: Design South Signage Div.
Consultant: Gibbs Landscaping

3, 5, 6. Clean lines of all entrance and exterior signing continue the crisp, modernist vocabulary of the architecture.
4. The building directory works as a sculptural element.
7. Concept and development sketches illustrate the evolution of sculptural signing elements.

3.

4.

5.

6.

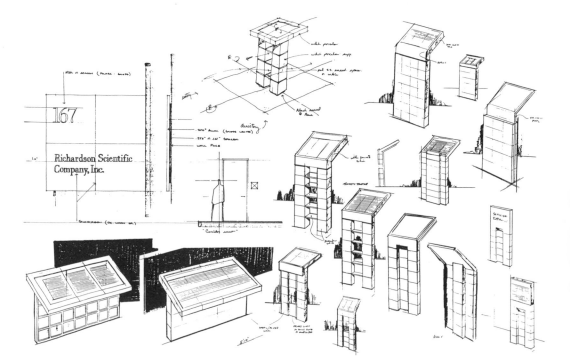

U.S. Army Corps of Engineers Sign Standards Program

Environmental graphics serve a host of purposes, ranging from directional and informative to purely illustrative and decorative. Occasionally, however, safety issues are foremost, and programs that address these factors bear a different importance, a greater weight purely by virtue of the responsibility they bear. Such was the case with the sign standards program developed for the U.S. Army Corps of Engineers, a comprehensive visual communications program designed to address legends, graphics, material specifications, and program-management process for 4500 recreation facilities, as well as a waterside safety sign system for all U.S. navigable waterways and rivers. Together, these locations host 500 million visitors annually.

In an effort "to create a more effective family of pictograms for signing," the designers adopted unchanged (except for borders) 13 of the most commonly-used of the now familiar and recognizable AIGA/DOT symbols and rendered the rest of their 102 new symbols, mostly an update of the National Park Service's 1965 recreation symbols, in the style of AIGA/DOT. A medium brown was used for all recreation signs in an effort to maintain a consistent palette among routed redwood signs and HDO plywood signs with retro-reflective faces. A variety of Helvetica typefaces have been used for maximum legibility.

Wood posts were specified for all recreational signs, most of which are constructed of high-density overlaid plywood or routed, clear-heart redwood

1.

1. *Routed redwood is used for standard identification signing.*
2. *Both symbols and lettering are used to signal waste dump stations.*

2.

with sign faces made of retro-reflective sheeting and computer cut legends. They are assembled using concealed or tamper-resistant hardwood in the constant war against vandalism.

To differentiate waterway sign systems—which use technology similar to that of large-scale highway signs—the designers employed a different color system that would at once be legible at dawn and dusk hours, while "retaining standard color associations for danger and warning": white on bright red for danger signs; black on chartreuse for warning signs; and white on medium blue for lock and navigation information and instructions. The *Casebook* jurors remarked on the strength of these warning signals, and commended the overall program for being hard-edged, clear, effective.

The entire program has been consolidated into a 540-page Sign Standards Manual which includes planning instructions, visual standards, signage specifications, and reference material for the specification, ordering, manufacturing, and maintenance of all signing. The jurors found the design standards established in it made for a visual program that achieved its high-performance safety objectives.

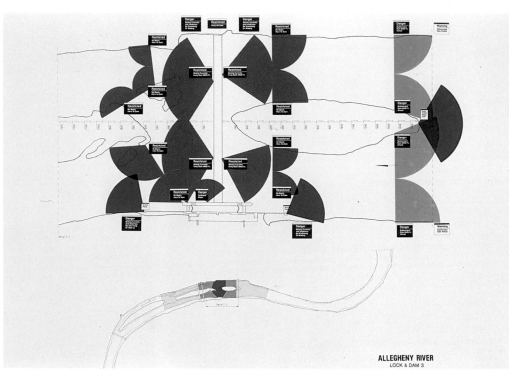

ALLEGHENY RIVER
LOCK & DAM 3

3.

3. A waterway safety sign zone system diagram (Pittsburgh, PA).
4. The program includes a series of new symbols based on AIGA/DOT system, some of which are for (left to right): gas station, viewing area, fish ladder, camp ground, drinking water, access, showers, wading area, canoeing, playground, hiking trail, horse trail.
5. The entire program is delineated in a comprehensive, 540-page, two-volume standards manual.

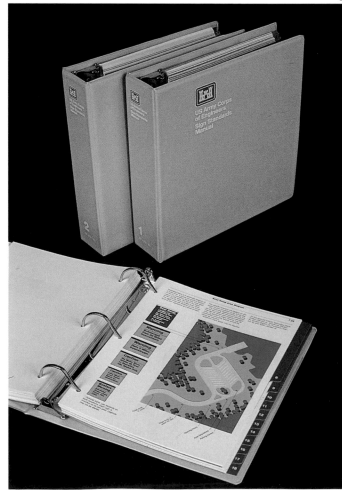

4.

5.

6.

7.

8.

9.

Client: U.S. Army Corps of Engineers, Washington, DC (Daniel O. Hileman, graphics coordinator).
Design firms: Meeker & Associates, Inc., New York City (beginning 1/1987); Meeker/Blum, Inc., New York City (10/85-12/86); Danne & Blackburn Associates, Inc., New York City (6/82-9/85)
Designers: Donald T. Meeker, Leslie Blum, Peter Reedijk, Kurt Jennings
Consultant: Paul Singer Design (symbol signs)
Fabricators: Southwood Corp. (routed redwood signs), APCO Graphics (office interior signs); System Graphics (cut graphics, screen printing, waterway signs).

6. A white-on-red color code is used for all waterway danger signs.
7. A black-on-chartreuse color code signals waterway warnings.
8. Symbol signs post prohibitions.
9. Program management forms and worksheets were also part of the graphics program.

Portland Center for the Performing Arts/New Theatre Building

1.

The interior and exterior signing program for the Portland Center for the Performing Arts/New Theatre Building achieves a delicate balance, managing to assert a sense of graphic authority without being too intrusive. "Because the architect requested that the signing be understated, we were designing to a minimum visual threshold," explains designer Michael Reed. Nevertheless, the architecture included expansive public spaces exposed to full-height glass curtain walls, where legibility posed obvious challenges under both daylight and artificial lighting conditions.

Studies demonstrated that "gold-leafed dimensional lettering was considerably more legible than expected," recalls Reed. That allowed the designers to down-size and modify letter spacing for a more elegant composition. The designers selected Futura Medium because they felt that when the typeface was used in all-caps with wide letterspacing, it reflected the character of the building. In fact, when viewing it at a distance, Reed believes, one has difficulty distinguishing whether or not the lettering is incised into the wood paneling or projecting from it.

Indeed, throughout the 36-month timetable of the program, the designers developed 27 assorted design elements for front and back of the house, all in stylistic synthesis with the architecture. In the public lobbies, for example, where dark cherrywood paneling had been specified, the designers found that etched-glass sign panels worked effectively

1, 2. Gold-leaf dimensional lettering with modified spacing establish a tone of understated elegance.
3. Both front and back surfaces of lobby floor directories were etched, creating an interplay of depth and shadow.
4, 5. Preliminary drawings developed letterspacing for entrance signing.

2.

3.

4.

5.

with background contrast. Throughout the program, etched glass, brass fixtures and sign cabinets, goldleaf and cast resin dimensional letterings all conform to the conventional, elegant vernacular of elegant concert halls and theatres. For the back of the house, designers specified fabricated aluminum sign panels and vinyl lettering.

Craftsmanship, materials, and finish were all objectives of the architecture. By assuming the same objectives, the designers created a graphics program that was in visual and tactile union with the building. Clearly, one way to sum it up might be to say that the program is a case of maximum elegance through a minimum visual threshold.

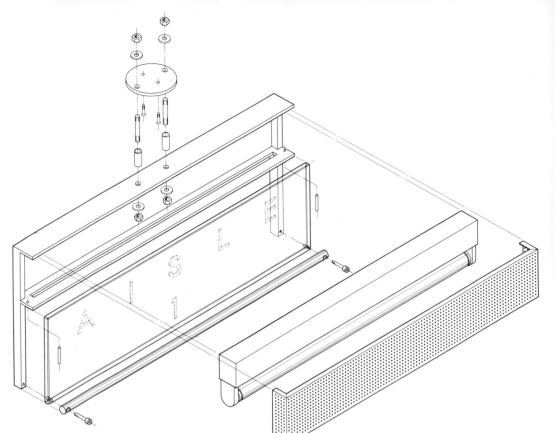

6.

7.

Client: City of Portland, OR
Design firm: Mayer/Reed, Portland
Designers: Michael Reed, project designer; Carey Sakai, assistant
Architect: Broome, Oringdolph, O'Toole, Rudolph and Associates; ELS Design Group; Barton Myers Associates
Fabricators: J. J. Quality Signs, cast resin characters, goldleaf work; Sidwell Fabrications, metal fabrication; Ostrom Co., etched-glass work; Pro-Ad-Co., screen printing; Lee's Better Letters, goldleaf work at entry doors and donor display

8.

6. *An exploded axonometric drawing illustrates the construction of illuminated signing.*
7-9. *The intense green edging of back-etched glass message panels works as a decorative element in itself.*

9.

Environmental Graphics/34

Carnegie Hall

Its eclectic neo-Renaissance architecture, formal auditorium, and celebrated acoustics have made New York's Carnegie Hall not simply a sublime music hall, but a cultural landmark as well. Maintaining it as such, and indeed, improving upon it, was the goal of the recent renovation by architects James Stewart Polshek and Partners. The restoration was a sensitive and informed effort to install contemporary mechanics and a more logical space flow without disrupting the building's original, resplendent architecture and acoustics.

Working within this agenda, Tracy Turner Design created a signing program—for lobby information such as box office-events, price information, and directional signs, as well as for box tier signs, restroom signing, and seating numbers—that was at once appropriate to the hall's ornate, original architecture *and* up-to-date, crisp, contemporary. Turner adapted Goudy Old Style with specially designed numerals as the predominant typeface to inject "elegance and liveliness to the system." In addition, she designed a wreath motif, suggestive of the building's architectural ornamentation, as a decorative accent for signing.

The elegant use of materials was cited at once by the *Casebook* jurors. Indeed, the traditional materials selected by Turner—gold leaf, glass, brass, and bronze, the last three selected for durability as well as visual appeal—all evoke a sense of style the old-fashioned way. Likewise, the burgundy and gold color theme suggests a classic, age-old, and practically regal sense of elegance.

1.

1. *The concert hall's ornate facade is shown here illuminated at night, revealing lobby areas involved in new signing program.*
2. *Burgundy background, sandblasted border, and mirror-polished gold leaf lettering were used on directional signs.*
3. *Box-office information signs can be rearranged as needed.*
4. *A wreath motif was used as an ornamentation throughout.*
5. *Changeable plastic box-office information signs can be easily rearranged.*
6. *Mirror-polished lettering was used in the lobby.*

2.

3.

4.

5.

6.

7.

8.

9.

Variations on the theme and further refinement have been achieved through surface finishes: satin-finished brass, sandblasted brass, mirror polishes, and burnished and unburnished gold leaf. For example, unburnished gold leaf, Turner explains, glows in dim light and was used on all box numbers and restroom signing. Plastics designed to imitate the better materials were used in the back of the house.

Working within a design budget of $35,000 to $50,000, the designers completed the project in 28 weeks. "It was an act of love," recalls Turner, "a thrill to be involved with such an intense, prestigious, and fast-paced project." It is a genuine respect and enthusiasm that the jurors agreed was reflected in the finished product.

Client: Carnegie Hall Corp., New York City
Design firm: Tracy Turner Design, Inc., New York City
Designers: Tracy Turner; Mary Elliott, senior designer; Ann K. Gustafson, administrative assistant
Architect: James Stewart Polshek and Partners
Fabricators: ASI Sign Systems, Inc.

7. *Mirror-polished brass elevator jamb signs include Braille.*
8. *Men's-room sign is constructed in gold leaf on glass with burgundy lettering.*
9. *Gold silkscreened border detail frames changeable displays for box-office events.*
10. *An axonometric drawing of the concert hall illustrates the scope of the signing program.*

10.

Playskool & Milton Bradley Showrooms

A mundane stretch of one of New York City's cross-town streets was enlivened when the 13 windows of a major toy-maker's showrooms blossomed with charming, larger-than-life paintings of children at play. The hand-painted panels and the flags with company names which fly above them during the annual two-week Toy Fair in February announce the presence of Hasbro, the world's largest manufacturer of toys and games.

Located in a registered historic cast-iron building on West 23rd Street are offices of the giant Pawtucket, Rhode Island, corporation as well as showrooms. Sussman/Prejza designers developed the visual solutions for graphics and toy display imagery and collaborated with the architectural firm of Barton Myers Associates, who had planned and designed the interiors of Hasbro's space.

The contents of the window panels, which ensure privacy for the interiors, are part of an ongoing graphic scene Sussman/Prejza first developed for Hasbro for the Vancouver World's Fair in 1985, based on photographs by Len Gittleman that symbolize the classical experience of children at play. In the treatment here, the paintings resembling abstract photographic figures in muted colors depict children involved with such traditional items as hoops, bicycles and teeter-totters rather than the "latest toys" which could disappear at any time.

Environmental product displays indoors support the product line. Displays have been organized chronologically

1. Flags with company names flown during the two-week Toy Fair in February announce Hasbro's presence at its New York City showrooms.

1.

and include "environments" for playthings designed for nursery-age infants as well as electronic strategy games for older children and adults. Such displays also work to impose a sense of coherence over the diverse design of the product lines.

For interior signing and product display, the designers developed a varied color palette, using at least 50 colors. As Sussman/Prejza designer Mark Nelsen explains, softer hues were used in areas for younger children, with stronger colors for older kids. Futura Demi typeface was chosen for "its simple, clean, geometric, and timeless style that worked well with the toys." The

2, 3. *Hand-painted window panels illustrate "Hasbro kids" at play.*
4. *All major interior signing was executed in anodized, color-tinted, etched aluminum.*
5. *The use of a clean, geometric typeface contrasts with the more playful typefaces used on children's products.*

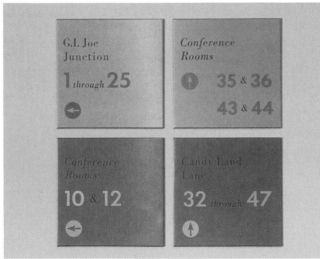

6. *A vibrant color palette and bold geometric accent shapes establish the tone for the Playskool showroom.*

7.

Casebook jurors concluded that the overall program both instilled a sense of visual coherence throughout the showrooms and conveyed an appropriate sense of a toy maker's products. Says Deborah Sussman, firm principal, "Hasbro's desire to involve itself with architecture, design and art in a significant way reflects its role as a serious corporation with a face toward Wall Street."

7, 8. Display environments in the Playskool showroom demonstrate products at work . . . or at play.

8.

Client: Hasbro, Inc., Pawtucket, RI
Architect and interiors: Barton Myers Associates
Color and graphics: Sussman/Prejza & Co., Inc., Santa Monica, CA
Designers: Deborah Sussman, Paul Prejza, Mark Nelsen, Kyoko Tsuge, James Barkley, Kristen Dietrich, Charles Milhaupt, Lance Glover, Susan Hancock
Window design: Deborah Sussman, Charles Reimers, Stephen Silvestri, designers; Len Gittleman, photographer

Environmental Graphics/40

Herman Miller Pavilion

Herman Miller has a variety of dealerships and showrooms around the country, including 30 independently-owned dealerships called Office Pavilions where its own products and those of its affiliated companies are sold. Herman Miller also owns 20 showrooms where only its products are shown but not sold. To augment all of these, Herman Miller decided to create an expanded pavilion near its Michigan headquarters where it would show its own

1.

products plus those of affiliated companies, and provide information about them via numerous techniques, including interactive video.

Located at company offices in Grandville, Michigan—halfway between the nearest airport in Grand Rapids and Herman Miller corporate headquarters, 40 miles to the southwest in Zeeland, Michigan—the pavilion is intended to reflect the latest in design and research for the office landscape, including lighting, acoustics and installation. It addresses a multitude of visitors— employees, sales personnel, dealers, customers, architects, and interior designers, to name only some.

This pavilion is not designed as a dealership for selling products, but more as a sales tool billing itself "an eclectic

2.

1. Main entrance leads to both pavilion and sales and marketing offices.
2. A medley of unevenly spaced letters at the pavilion's entrance conveys a sense of motion and activity.
3. An axonometric drawing illustrates the different functions and products exhibited at the pavilion.

Systems furniture

Seating products

Say Hello to the Owners exhibit

Neon at cafeteria entrance

Picnic exhibit in cafeteria

Pavilion entrance

Banners on both sides of esplanade

Pavilion sign

Esplanade

Building entrance

3.

feast of products, exhibits, and activities that invites a hearty sampling of Herman Miller." Included in the program for that sampling are a logo, signing, banners, a photographic exhibit, a neon wall graphic and a graphic timeline illustrating the company's history.

The logo, for example, a series of geometric shapes falling in place, conveys a sense of motion, activity. There is nothing static here, it seems to say. Similarly, the entrance sign, rendered in oversize, blocklike, painted aluminum letters, is a three-dimensional rendition of the logo. Herman Miller's in-house designers selected Helvetica Light caps: "We wanted it to be simple and not detract from the geometric shapes and the activity of the logo," they explain.

A series of brightly colored cotton banners draws visitors along an esplanade to the pavilion. Again, their design has been based on the letter shapes from the logo; but they are expressed here in the vibrant color palette developed for the entire program, in which turquoise, yellow-orange, magenta, and purple were selected as key colors. Exhibits displayed within the pavilion include a collage of photographs and images from the annual Herman Miller summer picnics and a pictorial timeline illustrating the company's history. Together, they convey a spirit of interaction throughout the Herman Miller community, a sense of community the company hopes will be infused in its greater circle of dealers, designers, and end users. The success of the Grandville Pavilion led to the opening of a second major pavilion at the company's West Coast manufacturing and sales headquarters in Irvine, California (Los Angeles).

Jurors were impressed with the overall vibrance of this first program, and especially with the varied applications of geometric shapes, finding their wit and whimsy effective. "Too often, banners just look like someone's been out hanging laundry," commented one juror. "Here, they've been hung like works of art and it works."

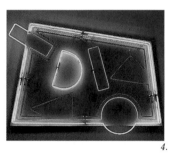

4.

5.

4. Neon graphic marks the cafeteria entrance.
5. Esplanade banners line the entrance to the pavilion.
6, 7. Preliminary banner sketches explore color palettes and shapes.

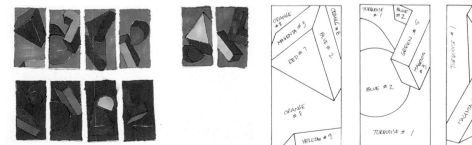

6.

7.

8.

9.

8. *Sales kits for pavilion include an information packet, bags, nametags, product resource cards, buttons, slide strips, and postcards.*
9. *A pavilion exhibit introduces visitors to Herman Miller employees.*
10. *A time line celebrating Herman Miller history familiarizes guests with the company's products.*
11. *Letter shapes falling into place make up the pavilion logo and suggest an atmosphere of activity.*
12, 13. *Early sketches investigate alternative logo proposals.*

Client: Herman Miller, Inc., Zeeland, MI
Design firm: Herman Miller, Inc., Zeeland
Designers: Linda Powell, art director; Barb Herman, graphic project manager; Sue Bakker, Marlene Capotosto, graphic production managers; Barbara Loveland, Kathy Stanton, Rob Hugel, Steve Frykholm, designers
Interior/exhibit design firm: Donovan & Green
Consulting architect: Daniel Brown & Associates
Fabricators: Valley City Sign Co.; Eby-Patrick Designs, Inc.

10.

PAVILION

HERMAN MILLER PAVILION

12.

13.

HERMAN MILLER 11.

43/Environmental Graphics

Sunrise Preschools

The multifaceted programs for Sunrise Preschools began with promotion of a single facility at a single location. "We were asked to develop a marketing plan, possibly using direct delivery, for a new school to be built in Tempe, Arizona," explain the designers, Richardson or Richardson, of Phoenix. With that in mind, they designed a format for building and vehicle signing and graphics in a gray, yellow, and white color palette.

As the marketing plan broadened to include new locations, the designers developed the signing program further, using shovel, saw, and key motifs, rendered in primary colors, to promote neighborhood awareness. Applied to a site trailer, the graphics made for an upbeat, positive image to introduce the preschool program in its early stages of construction. Augmenting the signing was the direct delivery of diecut cardboard tools with a printed message hung on the doors of 20,000 to 40,000 homes within the area of the new school site. The hundreds of calls that these "tools" elicited from interested parents are testimony to the program's success.

Finally, the "Extra Neat Stuff" phase, including whimsical illustrations developed for brochures and vehicle signing, promoted after-school programs in gymnastics, swimming, dance, computer, and foreign languages. "The idea," say the designers, "came as a result of the client's feeling that these programs needed to be promoted in a 'fun' and exciting manner. Since the programs are optional, we had to create a demand for enrollment."

For all its different phases and varied design components, the *Casebook* jurors found the graphics program "totally cohesive." Each step was consistent both with other steps of the program *and* with the

1.

We're building another
Sunrise Preschool. Call 878-6556

2.

Pace Corporation is building another
Sunrise Preschool. Call 265-3404.

Pace Corporation is building another
Sunrise Preschool. Call 265-3404.

3.

4.

1. *Freestanding building signing establishes the gray, yellow, and white color palette.*
2. *The marketing program includes site signing in the shape of a saw.*
3. *Vehicle signing continues saw and key motifs.*
4-6. *Color composition and other early drawings and mechanicals explore the application of various motifs.*

Sunrise Preschool

We're building another
Sunrise Preschool. Call 878-6556.

6.

5.

nature of preschool education.
The typeface used, for
example, was Century Oldstyle,
condensed by about 10 per cent
from normal character width.
Not only is it an extremely
readable typeface, but as
the designers explain, "The
face appears corporate-like
while still being somewhat
'elementary,' probably
because of the common
use of its ancestor, Century
Schoolbook, in children's
books and textbooks."

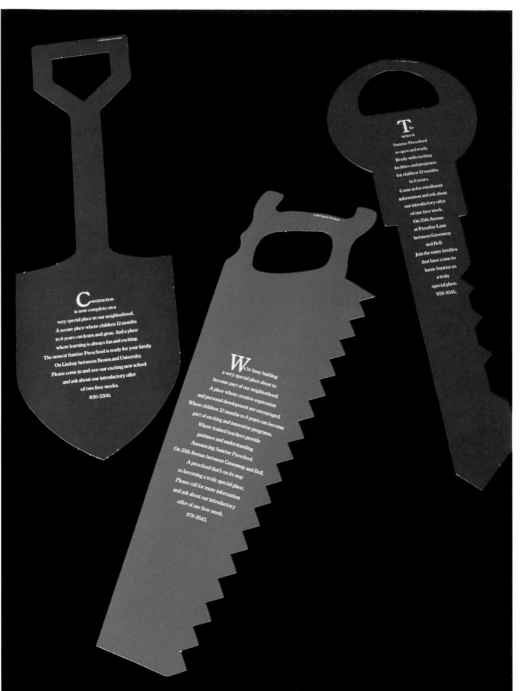

7.

8.

7, 8. Diecut shovels, saws, and keys hung on the doors of market area homes announce the construction of new schools.
9. Sunrise brochures announce different programs as they are offered.
10. "Extra Neat Stuff" vehicle graphics mechanical used for client approval and production coordination.
11. The "Extra Neat Stuff" van was painted in halves, in two of the secondary primary colors of the program (lavender and deep rose).

Environmental Graphics/46

Client: Sunrise Preschools, Scottsdale, AZ
Design firm: Richardson or Richardson, Phoenix
Designers: Forrest Richardson, art director; Valerie Richardson, art director; Rosemary Connelly, designer (site trailer); Jim Bolek, designer ("Extra Neat Stuff" van sign)

9.

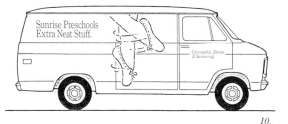

10.

11.

Barnett Plaza

As project director Richard Poulin explains, the objective of the environmental graphics program for Barnett Plaza was to make a strong connection with the architecture. The development in downtown Tampa included a 40-story office building, an 11-story garage, a health club, and a retail concourse, all constructed in the stark language of the International Style.

The exterior of the office building, distinguished by its ziggurat-like stepped-back profile, is sheathed in travertine marble with black granite and mirror-polished stainless steel. The interior finishes used in most of the building's public spaces include a reddish bronze, deep-red mahogany, and green and white marbles. In form and material alike, the design of the building is unembellished, clean.

The design criteria for the graphics program developed for tenant areas, parking garage, health club, public mall, and exterior signing conformed to this architectural vocabulary. As the designers, de Harak & Poulin of New York City, observe, "The majority of the architectural materials used on the building were reflected in the sign program, so that the signing would appear sensitive and integral to its environment." The *Casebook* jurors agreed that it was.

The predominant component in the program—achieved within a fabrication budget of between $275,000 and $300,000—was a panel sign produced in a variety of different sizes for different applications. The color palette selected was comprised of a warm gray (PMS 404C), the color used throughout the interior office environment, and green (PMS 349C), the predominant color in the architectural metal work in the garage. The designers also specified Helvetica typefaces in keeping with the International Style simplicity of the architecture. Likewise, the ziggurat profile of the building was also repeated in interior sconces.

The greatest problem confronting the designers during the 18-month project was the identification for the office building. The Barnett Bank, the major tenant and a large banking institution in the Southeast, has traditionally used rear-illuminated emerald-green lettering for its exterior signing. The designers felt that signs of this kind would correspond neither to the architecture nor to the remainder of the graphics program. Their solution? Ten-foot-high letters resembling travertine marble (actually painted sheet aluminum) that are internally lit in the evenings with neon, creating a halation of light around each individual letter.

The *Casebook* jurors were impressed by the overall restraint and elegance of such a comprehensive program. "It's simple, readable, and well-executed," said one. They remarked as well on the appropriate exterior use of the sans-serif typeface.

1.

2.   3.

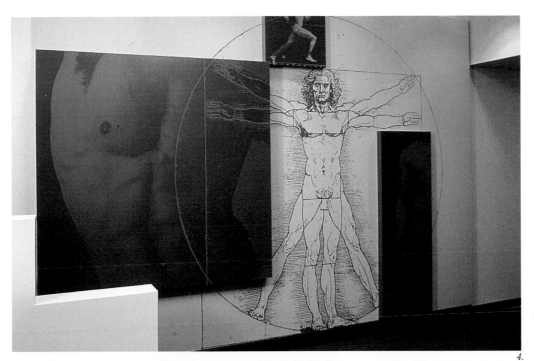

1. *Ten-foot-high painted sheet aluminum letters announce the 40-story office building.*
2, 3. *A panel sign system serves a variety of directional functions.*
4. *A DaVinci image of man signals the main entrance to the health club.*
5. *Sandblasted black granite is used for exterior signing.*
6. *Ziggurat-like ornamentation of fixtures reflects the building's own profile.*
7. *Sans-serif typefaces used in interior signing correspond to International Style simplicity.*

4.

5.

6.

3000

Paragon Group, Inc.

Licensed Real Estate Broker
Downtown Leasing

7.

Client: Paragon Group, Tampa, FL
Design firm: de Harak & Poulin Associates, Inc., New York City
Designers: Richard Poulin, project director/project designer; Kirsten Steinorth, project designer
Architect: Harwood K. Smith & Partners, Inc., Dallas
Fabricators: County Neon Sign Corp.; Signs & Decal Corp.; The Sign Co.

Kellogg Company Headquarters

It is perhaps predictable that the wheat motif was selected as the dominant visual theme for the Kellogg Company's corporate headquarters. Themes of grains and harvesting, and by association, good health and prosperity, are all in keeping with the image the company hopes to project. Less predictable, however, was the wide range of creative applications for the motif, and the extensive art collections used to fully express it.

The designers—Hellmuth, Obata & Kassabaum (St. Louis)—have made a point of representing the theme not just through surface embellishment, but through architectural ornamentation of all sorts, using polished bronze, wood, etched and leaded glass, and textiles. Etched-glass clerestories, for example, have been patterned with a stylized wheat motif, while at the entry to the board room, leaded glass panels pick up the same pattern. Inlaid woods in the atrium and on the bridges, as well as textured carpeting and rugs, continue the motif. And in the food counter section, the servery, of the corporate dining facility, forged

1.   2.   3.   4.   5.

6.

1-5. Interior details in a variety of materials repeat the wheat motif.
6. Leaded glass panels frame the entrance to the board room.

7.

*7. Bas-relief entryway decoration
establishes the theme of harvest and
prosperity.*
*8, 9. The wheat motif has been freely
adapted in a variety of wall treatments.*

8.

9.

10. *An exhibit of company history has been installed in the gallery.*
11. *Forged iron ornamentation is used in the servery.*

11.

iron and patterns in wall tile suggest specific foods.

Crafts have been used here, not as showcase items, but as a design process integral to the architecture of the building. The *Casebook* jurors especially praised the consistently high level of craftsmanship in the different materials, finding that, despite the prominence of the theme, there is a sense of restraint rather than extravagance. While the image has certainly been repeated, it is not redundant. Overkill, so often the convention in the expression of corporate image, is noticeably, and thankfully, absent here.

More unusual still, perhaps, is the further expression of the theme through collections of sculpture, art, and photographs supervised and positioned by the design team. Bas-relief

terra-cotta panels by Courtney Bean, with forms inspired by grains and foodstuffs, frame office area entries. Displayed throughout the office areas is a collection of photographs depicting sowing, reaping, and the bringing to market and preparation of foods. Tapestries and Amish quilts ornament reception and executive dining rooms. Finally, four large sculptures have been commissioned, as has an expansive bronze bas-relief wall-piece for the atrium depicting the agricultural landscapes of Missouri, Illinois, and Kansas as seen from the air.

"The genesis of all the interior design was found in expressing Kellogg's connections to the land and fundamental values of good nutrition," explain the designers. And indeed, the

program suggests a sense of bounty, plenitude. But the impression made by this environmental graphics program is also one of a collaboration of spirit, a collaboration that includes not only the architects, designers, and clients, but the broader circle of artists and craftspeople whose work has been used. While not all of the work has been specially commissioned, of course, what is shown suggests a likemindedness among a diverse group of participants. And by using the work of so many artists and craftspeople, the designers have expressed the theme not as a single, corporate value, but as a more universal, human set of values. This is what infuses the program with its greater meaning and its strong presence.

Client: Kellogg Co., Battle Creek, MI
Design firm/architect: Hellmuth, Obata & Kassabaum, St. Louis
Designers: Charles P. Reay, senior designer, environmental graphics; Gyo Obata, architecture; Cicely Drennan, project designer, artworks; Kathy Gregory, project designer, graphics; Debby Fitzpatrick, Louise Angst, signing; Scott Hueting, exhibits
Fabricator: ASI, signing; Davlon Co., sculpture; Ken Lieberman, photographic artworks; Don Asbee, servery

Pacific Design Center (Phase 2)

Like other design marketplaces around the country, the Pacific Design Center in West Hollywood not only accommodates top-of-the-line furniture and furnishings showrooms, but is an architectural showcase of sorts in itself. The immense blue-glass structure designed a decade ago by architect Cesar Pelli has recently been joined by a nine-story building of green spandrel glass, and planned for the future is a building in the form of a huge red wedge.

The three-phase building project has been accompanied by a three-phase, color-coded graphics program by the Sussman/Prejza design firm that includes garage graphics, directional signs, sculptural graphics, computer directories, and an electronic message center. As the designers point out, "The signage program took its design direction from the architecture. The buildings were very strong, bold geometric statements, and our graphics reflected that boldness in simple geometric shapes and limited colors."

Much of the signing, then, constructed for the most part of painted aluminum and fiberglass, takes the form of oversize cubes, spheres, triangles, tilting squares and rectangles, all of which add up to an assertive directional program. Much of its effect comes from its spatial, three-dimensional quality, clearly not the norm in most signing programs. With yellow as the thread common to all three buildings, the designers have used the building colors themselves as signals for each building. Directory arrows,

1.

1, 2. The strong geometric shapes and bright colors of the signing program take their cues from the building's architecture.

2.

3. *Phase Two of the Design Center—an immense green, chamfered glass cube (left). Phase One's building at right is joined to second building by low blue glass section in foreground.*
4. *A sculptured directional arrow is color-coded.*
5-7. *Early study models were built to determine the scale and placement of directional devices.*

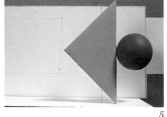

4.

5.

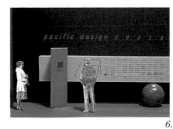

6.

7.

8. Typefaces are Univers 58 and 76, chosen for the strong impact they make when combined.
9. Bright yellow was established as the common color thread for directional devices for all three buildings.

8.

for example, are green or blue (and some will eventually be red) depending on where visitors are being directed.

Informational graphics that are not specific to any of the buildings have been rendered in yellow. The use of Univers typeface furthers the simple, bold theme of the program without undermining its impact.

The designers, at least in part, credit the success of the program to the synthesis of effort behind it, citing "a strong graphic direction that was not diluted by committee but supported through collaboration." And indeed, the jurors applauded the program, agreeing that its assertive colors and shapes not only complemented the architecture of the marketplace but, more indirectly, reflected the unrestricted spirit of Southern California as well.

Client: Pacific Design Center, West Hollywood, CA
Design firm: Sussman/Prejza & Co. Inc., Santa Monica, CA
Designers: Deborah Sussman, Paul Prejza, Scott Cuyler
Architect: Cesar Pelli and Associate
Fabricator: Ampersand Contract Signing; Gene Siegrist Studio

9.

IDCNY

When the first-completed section of the International Design Center New York in Long Island City opened its doors for business in the fall of 1985, one of its chief objectives was to give New Yorkers a design resource comparable to those found in Chicago, Los Angeles, and Houston, to name only a few of the cities that were ahead of New York in offering their residents a large-scale furnishings marketplace. The four structures, covering a 10-acre site, have been designed in phases, and Centers One and Two, now complete, offer a total of one-million square feet of showroom space.

As in any such design center, however, the multitude and sheer diversity of showrooms can provoke a sense of visual cacophony and overload. Add the fact that the immense scale of such spaces can tend to be confusing or disorienting, and the challenge to the program for architectural graphics becomes clear. Predictably, Vignelli Associates did not flinch from the task—which, in this case, included rooftop project identification, traffic signing, parking pylons, building identification, illuminated and non-illuminated directory pylons, elevator directories, fire-code signs, restroom and telephone signs, and service door identification.

"The architects' color palette was very monochromatic and neutral," the designers observe. "Signs are bright red, so they stand out in the large space. By restricting the color to red, red becomes a signal for information."

While the color palette may have been limited, its applications were not. Begin, for example, with the towering 32'-high aluminum letters, in a vivid baked-enamel red, positioned on the rooftop of IDCNY. Already a visual landmark in Long Island City,

1. Thirty-two-foot-high aluminum letters positioned at rooftop level work as an urban beacon.

1.

the letters act as a beacon of sorts for travelers from Manhattan, across the East River, who consider themselves pioneers in the urban frontier of Queens. Likewise, aluminum traffic signs, also in red baked-enamel, and steel parking pylons with red porcelain enamel work as clear pathmarkers.

Interior signing and directories, also steel with red porcelain enamel, have been silkscreened with white type. Bodoni Bold and Bodoni Bold Italic (limited to directory sublistings) were selected for simplicity and readability. Strategically positioned, they do not conflict with or try to compete against or "outdesign" individual showroom graphics. Rather, standing out in the expansive space by virtue of their color, the signs quickly establish their own visual authority and clearly direct visitors to the assorted buildings, floors, and showrooms. The *Casebook* jurors were understandably impressed with the crisp elegance and overall clarity of the signing program.

Client: International Design Center New York, Long Island City, NY
Design firm: Vignelli Associates, New York City
Designers: Massimo Vignelli; Rebecca Rose, vice president/architectural graphics; Janice Carapellucci, senior designer
Architect: Gwathmey Siegel & Associates
Associated architect: Stephen Lepp Associates
Fabricator: Signs and Decal

2.

2. Fifteen-inch letters pin-mounted to canopies are used for building identification.
3. Steel parking pylons are coated with red porcelain enamel.
4, 5. A code for all building information is established through the use of color in interior signing.
6. White silkscreened type applied to red porcelain enamel makes for a crisp, readable effect.

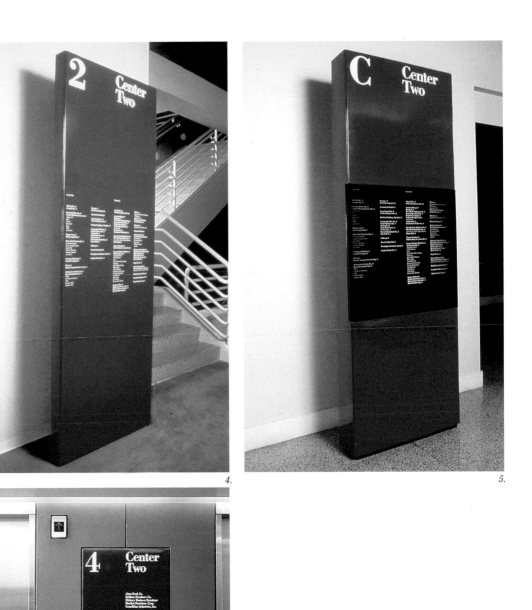

4.

5.

6.

3.

Children's Hospital
& Medical Center

1.

2.

1-3. All exterior signing is based on a system of panels mounted on rounded aluminum support posts.

3.

If the medical environment generates a sense of apprehension among adults, it is more likely to nurture genuine fear and intimidation among children. Addressing these negative perceptions was the graphics program designed for Children's Hospital & Medical Center in Seattle. As the designers explain, their program met two objectives: "The client requested that the final solution have elements of playfulness that would reflect the institution's mission as a children's hospital, and at the same time communicate a feeling of competence and corporate order."

Executed in three years at a cost of $95,000, the program included the design of exterior site labels, directional signs, parking-lot labels, traffic-control signs, interior directories, directional and destinational signs, room labels, and code and life safety signs.

The designers, from TRA Graphics Design, Seattle, felt that Benguiat Gothic Bold type would interject an appropriate sense of playfulness. Rounded support posts, moreover, work to "soften the corporate influences in the design criteria and provide a bridge from the roundness of the typeface to the rigid geometry of the sign panels."

The entire signing system was based on modular proponents, with exterior signs fabricated from Alucobond composite material and structural aluminum tube. Graphics are surface-applied reflective vinyl lettering. Interior signing is constructed

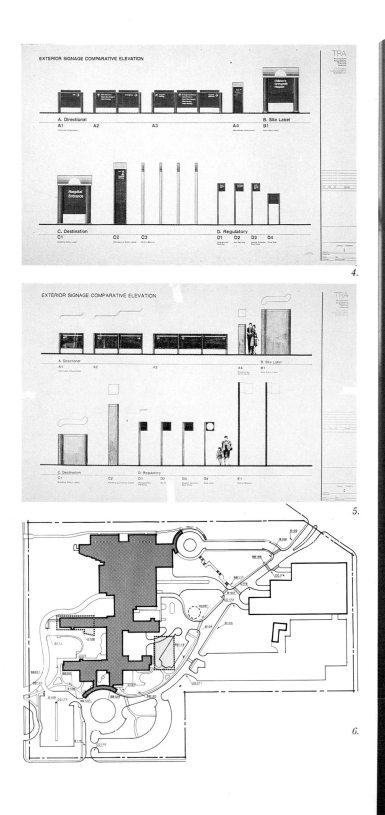

4, 5. *Preliminary drawings investigate early style alternatives.*

6. *A site plan suggests the scope of the exterior signing program.*

7. *Exterior scale models were constructed to investigate color, scale, typography and form.*

from plywood with custom aluminum edge trim pieces and end caps, and shares with exterior signing a common, crisp color palette of blue and white. Interior directional signs use the "cartoon bubble," a staple of juvenile language and literature that was adopted for its obvious lighthearted touch.

The *Casebook* jurors called the typeface effective and the overall program "friendly." Indeed, if the medical environment is one generally perceived by children as hostile and threatening, this program makes an effort to redress that image.

8.

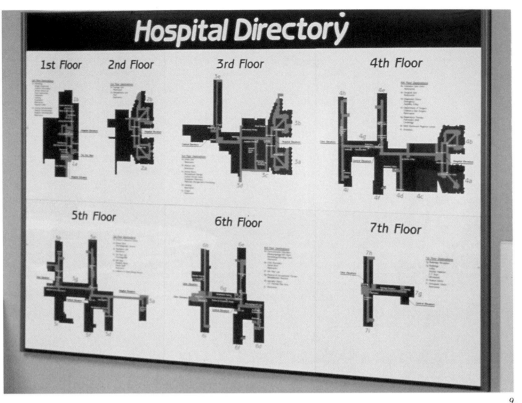

9.

8. Changeable panels were used for interior directional signing.
9. An interior building directory guides visitors throughout the seven floors. A hospital-conducted survey showed an 85 per cent favorable reaction to the new signing program.
10. The cartoon-bubble format of interior department destination labels have an element of playfulness appropriate to a children's hospital.

Client: Children's Hospital & Medical Center, Seattle
Design firm: TRA Graphic Design, Seattle
Designers: Kelly Brandon, Jon Bentz, Virginia Newman, Mike Marshall
Fabricators: Popich Signs Co., Meyer Sign Co., The Graphics Co.

10.

11. Blue panels with white graphics used for signing contrast with the vivid color palette of the interior.
12. Signing for patient wards can be easily revised.
13. Elevator code signing.
14. A panel-additions system is flexible and can be changed easily.
15. Patient chart and information units allow for quick revisions.

11.

12.

13.

14.

15.

City of Cincinnati
Uptown Neighborhoods

The most challenging locale for the environmental graphic designer is the urban landscape. Producing graphics that are noticeable, much less informative, amidst the entrenched clutter and jumble of street furniture and signs is a formidable task. Such efforts all too frequently result in a worsening of the visual overload. However, the *Casebook* jurors found a notable exception to the norm in the signing program for the "Uptown" Cincinnati neighborhoods.

The program was designed to unify six neighborhoods in Cincinnati and to identify three different types of facilities in these areas: medical, educational/research/ recreational, and commercial. "With a population of about 71,000 and a work force in excess of 30,000, this area has Greater Cincinnati's second highest concentration of residential, commercial, and institutional activity," explains Robert Probst of Schenker, Probst, Barensfeld, one of the two Cincinnati design firms involved.

Working with a panel made up of city architects and designers, traffic engineers, planners, and business and institutional representatives, the designers established the criteria for the project: to resolve the lack of clear, directional signing; to address the lack of emergency information to medical facilities; and to clarify confusing institutional and business signing already displayed in the multi-use area.

The designers began by creating what they call "a

1.

2.

3.

1. Contrasting colors are used to indicate the different types of facilities of the multi-use area—in this case, medical and institutional.
2. Blue—PMS 312—was used for all hospital identification.
3. Brown—PMS 167—was used for all business district identification.

5.

6.

7.

4. Color coding makes the signing for the three different types of facilities easily recognizable.
5-7. Preliminary sketches investigate the use of banners as well as color-coded panel signs.

distinct, kinetic identity mark" composed of upward-slanting color-coded bands, and a logo, the single word "Uptown." The color code was then continued in the signing, with blue (PMS 312) signaling hospitals, green (PMS 376) for institutions and public facilities, and brown (PMS 167) for commercial.

Materials specified included black-steel structures and silkscreened semi-gloss black aluminum signfaces. Typefaces used were Frutiger 56 and Frutiger 66, both modified by an additional five-degree slant for increased readability to motorists.

Considering the design budget of $30,000 and production and installation costs of $100,000—or approximately $1000 per sign—the jurors agreed that the system provided a cost-effective and expedient signing program. Its application, moreover, could be extended to phone booths, benches, trash receptacles, kiosks, banners, and other assorted street furniture as the city budget permits.

The designers admit that the slow pace of the approval process from the city presented problems—research began in 1982, and the first signs were erected in 1987. Nevertheless, in retrospect, they credit the program's success to the team effort that included the inevitable city bureaucracy.

One of the results of the project, Probst notes, was being able to "follow our own signs to work everyday through heavy traffic." This, he says, was most gratifying.

8, 9. Early drawings determine letterspacing and angle of Uptown mark. *10.* An early drawing examines sign construction.

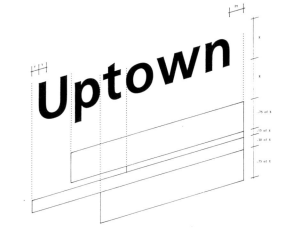

The Uptown Mark   1

Letterspacing and Angle

The Uptown Mark consists of the word 'Uptown' placed above four upward slanting bars.

The word 'Uptown' is always set in modified Frutiger 66 and spaced as shown.

The word 'Uptown' and the four slanting bars are always placed at an angle of 16½°. This places the vertical strokes of the letters perpendicular to horizontal.

Uptown Signage Project
Uptown Design Team, Cincinnati   8

The Uptown Mark   2

Bar Placement and Dimensions

The slanting bars must conform in width, length and placement to the specifications shown.

Uptown Signage Project
Uptown Design Team, Cincinnati   9.

Sign Construction   6

The graphic elements are white reflective material, silk screened, die-cut and applied to the sign face.

The Uptown Mark

Typography: die-cut and silk screened to match PMS 422

Bars: silk-screened and die-cut as one piece
Colors as specified

Message Band

White reflective material
Silk screened
Color as specified
Typography: reverses to white

Arrow die-cut and applied to message band

Uptown Signage Project
Uptown Design Team, Cincinnati   10.

11. *Early sketches develop color and typography.*
12. *Early sketches of upward slanting identity mark and its possible applications.*
13. *Sketches study application of signing system to common pieces of street furniture.*
14. *Sketches develop signing on panels of varying size and proportion.*

Client: City of Cincinnati, Dept. of Neighborhood Housing and Conservation
Design firm: "Uptown Design Team," joint venture of Chuck Byrne Design and Schenker, Probst, Barensfeld, Cincinnati
Designers: Chuck Byrne, Michael Overton/Chuck Byrne Design; Robert Probst, Heinz Schenker/Schenker, Probst, Barensfeld
Architect: Bob Richardson, Dept. of Architecture, City of Cincinnati
Fabricator: Hall Signs, Inc.
General contractor: Langenheim and Thomson Co.

Godzilla's Oriental Food Restaurant

Imagery for Godzilla's, a small oriental restaurant in Seattle relying largely on take-out and deliveries, was centered on that familiar figure in children's literature, the friendly monster. As the designer explains, the client wanted to appeal to all ages with the imagery, so if there was to be a monster, it could not be one frightening to children. In addition to the monster, the store ID included the hand-lettered name of the restaurant and information the client wanted to stress—"free delivery" and "oriental food to go." Legibility to passing motorists and easy recognition were also design criteria. All of these elements were to be

applied to the building's awning, the delivery truck, food containers, paper bags and T-shirts.

Designer Nancy Stentz searched first for a letterform that was "chunky, scaly, etc.," one that would lend itself to a "Godzilla look." The letterform she settled on generated immediate positive response. "It was everything we had worked for—individual, bold, eye-catching, and 'fun'." Budget restrictions (an $800 design budget and $3000 for all signing) dictated that the design be limited to three colors—a vivid green (PMS 563) for the monster; dark blue (PMS 547) for the "Godzilla" lettering and

1.

2.

1. The message of "Free Delivery" promotes the friendly image of the monster.
2. Graffiti on the side of the building is, for once, appropriate.
3. Readability to passing motorists determined the eye-catching logotype.
4-6. The logotype was also affixed to food containers and packaging, the delivery truck, and sweat shirts.

3.

4.

5.

6.

border on the circular monster "bug"; and a warm red for additional lettering as well as for the flashing electrical bolts radiating from the monster's jaws.

The startling message that "King Kong eats here" was added afterwards both as an attention-grabber and to use the blank side wall. "Great graffiti," concluded one *Casebook* juror. "Classic," added another.

Client: Wayne Palmer, Seattle
Design firm: Nancy Stentz Design, Seattle
Fabricator: Atlas Awning
Sign painter: Richard Webbinger

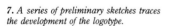

7. A series of preliminary sketches traces the development of the logotype.

7.

Norway Pavilion at EPCOT Center

While many of the graphics programs in this year's *Casebook* submissions were singled out by the jurors for accurately reflecting the architecture they accompanied, or the region in which they were located, the program for the Norway Pavilion was applauded for its evocative representation of an entire country. A big bill, to be sure. Formally introduced as "Norway, Gateway to Scandinavia," the 58,000-square-foot pavilion is the 11th national participant in the Epcot Center World Showcase at Walt Disney World, Florida. As sources for the pavilion explain, "A picturesque courtyard is the heart of the new pavilion surrounded by replicas of traditional Norwegian architecture—a 14th-century Akershus Castle, an ancient wooden stave church, red-roofed cottages from Bergen, and timber-sided farm buildings typical of the Nordic woodlands."

The program, then, had numerous objectives, among them to visually integrate the diverse architectural types; to communicate the concept of each building, its shops, restaurants, and exhibits; and to project an accurate sense of the country's history and cultural heritage. Components of the program included 10 marquees, menu stanchions, operational signs, atmospheric graphics, descriptive plaques, sculptural elements, exhibit graphics, and exit signs.

The Walt Disney Imagineering Company worked with a Norwegian civil-engineering and construction firm, commercial banks, shipping firms, and industrial groups, to name only some of the collaborators, to ensure both authenticity and financing. And designers on the Disney Imagineering team relied on the input of Norwegian architects and historians.

Working from architectural and interior drawings, landscape and lighting plans, as well as photo documentation of Norwegian architecture and graphics, the designers established the sensibility they were trying to create. Explains designer Mimi Sheean, "You could call Norwegian design Northern European eclectic." It has a rustic and rough-hewn quality, neither refined nor delicate, but heavier, more handcrafted. A color palette of dark tones and grays was established.

"The material sense,"

1, 2. Examples of traditional generic Norwegian architecture create an atmosphere of authenticity.

3-5, 9, 10. *Signing in a variety of typefaces conforms to a folk-art theme.*
6-8. *Graphic elements that suggest handcarved woodworking announce the Fjording, housing a variety of merchandise shops.*

11. *Rustic woodworking motifs are used at the entrance to the bakery.*
12. *Exterior signing reinforces the handcrafted, rustic image of the pavilion.*

9.

10.

11.

12.

continues Sheean, "was of lots of stone, brick, wood." While it was obviously impractical to duplicate these materials, the designers suggested them through the use of plexiglass, wood, sheet and cast aluminum, wrought iron, and fiber-reinforced plastic—all materials that are durable and weather-resistant, a genuine concern in the unpredictable Florida climate. A variety of typefaces was used, including Richmond Old Style and Romic, as well as some custom or modified faces, with the criterion for their selection being a sense of authenticity and legibility.

The *Casebook* jurors agreed that the designers' execution of the Nordic theme—completed within an 18-month schedule—was indeed genuine, calling the signing "well-crafted." "This is wholly appropriate for what it is," concluded one.

Client: Walt Disney Imagineering, Glendale, CA
Design firm: Walt Disney Imagineering
Designers: Greg Paul, Mimi Sheean, Anne Tryba
Architect: Ron Bowman
Interior designer: Tori McCullough
Fabricators: General Display; Walt Disney World Sign Shop; Graphic Solutions

13, 14. Graphics for the Maelstrom ride exploit the theme of Viking sea adventure.
15, 16. Reproductions of wrought-iron ornamentation embellish signing for the Akershus Restaurant.
17. Reproductions of primitive wood planking and carvings are used at the facade of the Puffin Roost that houses additional shops.

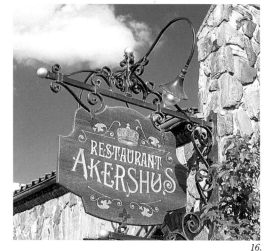

13.

14.

15.

16.

17.

Staten Island Children's Museum

The appeal of the signing program for this children's museum is obvious from the start: Pictorial hand-signals relay a wealth of information in a clear, original vocabulary that can be easily understood both by the children whom the museum exhibits address and their adult guides.

It is, however, the broad application of this imagery throughout the four floors of the museum that makes it especially engaging. The signing uses "hands and gestures to point, wave, and describe floor numbers," explain the designers (from Works in New York City). This, of course, describes the common body language used most by small children. The second floor, then, is indicated by a hand with two fingers raised; the direction of museum offices is indicated by a clerical-looking plexiglass hand with a wristwatch and a pen; and at the entrance, waving hands greet museum visitors. Hinges on fingers are a simple mechanism—in keeping with the simplicity of the overall program—that allows for variations on the theme.

Variety of applications is matched by a variety of materials: Formica and green chalkboard are used for directories, Formica and Lucite for hanging signs, Formica and brushed aluminum for small area signs, and neon for the waving window signs. Materials were selected both with regard to cost—the overall design budget was limited to $35,000—and with regard to changing exhibits and events. Simple eyescrews, for example, are the support system for hanging signs, a solution which

1.

1. Beckoning hands at the entrance both welcome visitors and introduce the theme used indoors.

the *Casebook* jurors found both imaginative and appropriate. For clarity and readability, the Akzidenz-Grotesk typeface of the museum's logo and stationery was used throughout.

A primary color code comprised of yellow, red, lavender, and blue indicates floor numbers, and is supplemented by a palette of blacks, browns, grays, and greens. In the realm of children's design—so often patronizing and obscure for the very audience it is meant to address—this signing program, based upon sign language and hand gestures, is indeed articulate, witty, lively, and above all, informative. All of which, of course, reflects the spirit of the museum itself.

2.

3.

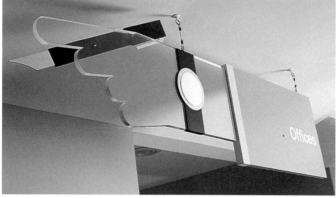

4.

5.

6.

7.

8.

2-7. Hand gestures relay a wealth of information including changing exhibits, floor numbers, directional information, and the location of coatroom and restrooms.
8. The neutral color palette used for the interior of the museum promotes a lively contrast with exhibits and signing.
9. The promotional program includes business cards, letterhead, and notepaper.

Client: Staten Island Children's Museum, Staten Island, NY
Design firm: Works, New York City
Designer: Keith Godard, Mark Donnolo
Architect: Hannigan & Prendegast
Consultant: David Ablon, Neon Design Associates
Fabricators: Gary Faro & Wayne Walker

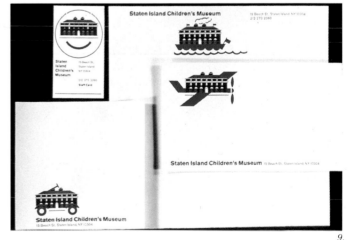

9.

Fake Billboards

1.

1, 4. Familiar '50s billboard vernacular is the language common to all of Johnson's humorous signing, including these two winning Casebook entries.
2. "Plates" was an early Johnson effort.
3. Artist makes detailed drawings ahead of time, but "doesn't always follow them."

"New York is a pretty humorless place these days. Maybe this helps," says Jerry Johnson of Orange Outdoor Advertising. And, indeed, Johnson's self-promotion billboards cannot help but humor even the most jaded urbanites. For almost a decade, drawing upon the familiar street jargon of the urban environment, the billboards have succeeded each other—one painted every year—on the wall of a four-story building in Brooklyn. They are rendered in the style of '40s and '50s advertising, and, at a cursory glance, that's just what they are taken for. The message, however, is more oblique. "Insist upon plates," suggested one that allegedly represented the National Clay Board. "They make every meal a special meal."

Johnson is a painter who makes a living painting outdoor advertisements, including a number of high-profile billboards, for real clients. The periodically changing message in this particular series, however, has taken the false claims of advertising to a new level of the fantastic, if not surreal. Rendered in synthetic enamels and oils and completed in four or five days, the 20'-by-25' ads have hawked everything from Metro ElectricCo and its symbol of friendly electricity, Reddy Kilowatt ("Imagine life without him . . . Pretty bleak, eh? So don't be stupid when you get your monthly power bill. Pay it immediately. And pay it gladly"), to the President's Council on Appearances ("Dress right . . . and get a better shake out of life"). Falling within the time-frame of this *Casebook* were two winners, Metro Electrico and Cash ("Rediscover the buying power of cash. It's always appropriate").

Explains Johnson, "This once-a-year project keeps me from going nutty with the type of work I do the other 51 weeks a year." The jurors agreed that such episodes of visual wit may keep the rest of us sane, too. And that their appeal is universal. "There's a place in life for this," sighed one, appreciatively.

2.

3.

4.

Design firm: Orange Outdoor Advertising, Brooklyn, NY
Designer: Jerry Johnson

ON FIFTH AVENUE ... AROUND THE W

Despite the positive public-relations role that successful construction barricades can play, their design usually begins with a disadvantage. Other graphic and signing programs may intend to direct, clarify, or simply brighten the way, often going hand-in-hand with a refined architectural program. The very premise of construction barricades, however, is to guide one through what is invariably an inconvenient mess. Those who are to be directed or otherwise influenced by such signing have already been inconvenienced and can be predisposed toward profound irritation. How better to address these irritations than with humor?

H. Stern Jewelers
Humor was precisely the objective of the construction barricade designed by Luckett & Associates for H. Stern Jewelers at 50th Street and Fifth Avenue in New York City. The photo mural consisted of oversize, black-and-white photos of actual construction workers, mounted on masonite boards for the sake of durability. The workers were

2.

ORLD, WE ADD COLOR.

bedecked, however, with handcolored gemstones one would be more likely to find on Princess Di. The wild incongruity of the image invariably amused passersby. Where else might one find a carpenter in overalls with pearls hanging from his pocket, a female construction worker in a hard hat and emerald earrings or a Yankees fan with a cigar and a $5000 watch from Patek Phillipe? Three additional images were created for an enclosed hallway leading to rear elevators that took customers to the second floor, where

display and sales areas had been relocated.

Aside from piquing humor, the barricade piqued curiosity. Because construction in the jeweler's first-floor showroom was to last for several months, the purpose of the barricade was to inform pedestrians that the store was still open for business. That this objective was met was clear in the store's sales figures. As the designers explain, "Although walk-in traffic dropped, a number of new customers who had never visited the store were introduced to the store and its products."

The *Casebook* jurors were unanimously engaged and amused by "the grand incongruity" of the images, agreeing that the designers' intent "to create an informative, appealing, humorous visual that was consistent with the store's marketing image as world leaders in the design and sale of colored gemstones" had been achieved.

Client: H. Stern Jewelers, New York City
Design firm: Luckett Associates, Venice, CA
Designers: Wes Neal, John Luckett
Architect: Karplus & Nussbaum

1.

1, 2. Exterior photomurals of bejeweled construction workers are echoed in photos lining interior corridor that skirted the renovation work requiring a construction barricade at H. Stern Jewelers on New York's Fifth Avenue.

712 Fifth Avenue

There is a similar tongue-in-cheek quality to Vignelli Associates' design solution for another construction barricade on New York's Fifth Avenue. Say the designers, "Basically, the idea was to create a delightful visual diversion for passersby, while providing some information about the building going up behind the barricade." The delightful diversion, in this case, was provided by an oversize blueprint of the two historic facades behind the barricade. The red strip below the blueprint with white vinyl lettering gave information about the project, while an immense, tilting yellow square gave the project name.

The simplicity of materials, including painted MDO plywood and corrugated fiberglass, and the use of primary colors, along with the selection of Helvetica Bold Condensed typeface, altogether made for simple, recognizable supergraphics signing with high impact. What made the greatest impact, perhaps, was the tilt and angle at which the yellow square slipped into the "blueprint," giving it a sense of dimension. The yellow square faced the flow of traffic without projecting into the street and being a danger to oncoming buses.

It was the designers' hope to create "a visible announcement for a new building in one of the world's most prestigious neighborhoods, turning what could be an eyesore into an asset for the developer, and indeed, the entire area." The *Casebook* jurors agreed that the hope had been amply fulfilled, remarking especially on the

4.

5.

dynamic scale and color of the barricade, finding it at once lively, expressive, and informative. Of undeniable appeal as well was the sense of theater that the "blueprints" infused into the construction: The building was veiled, hidden, mysterious. And the moment at which the finished facade was revealed brought an inevitable sense of drama.

Client: Solomon Equities, Inc., New York City
Design firm: Vignelli Associates, New York City
Design team: Massimo Vignelli, Rebecca Rose, Michael Leone, Stephen Magner
Architect: Kohn Pederson Fox Associates and Beyer Blinder Belle
Painter: Evergreene Painting Studios, Inc.

3. Blueprints rendered in the actual scale of the architecture work as an atypically informative construction barrier at 712 Fifth Avenue.
4, 5. A photograph with an overlay was used in early stages of design.
6-8. Elevations and detail drawings determine the final scale and relationship of different components.

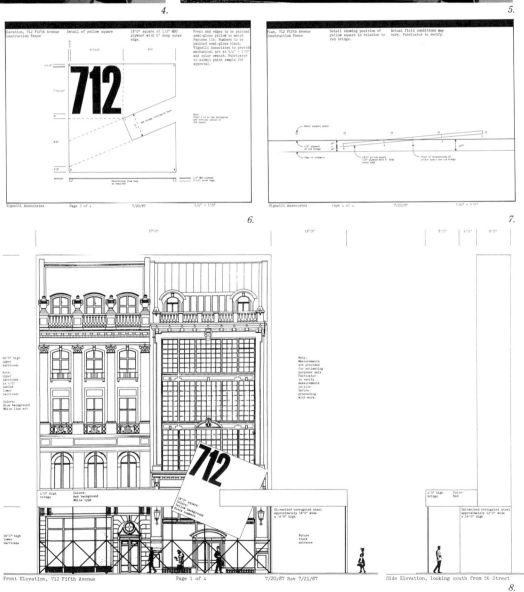

6.

7.

8.

California
Self Storage

1.

The vernacular roadside architecture of Southern California isn't what it should be, considering all the time which residents of the state spend on the freeways. The Santa Monica design firm of Sussman/Prejza has done its bit to rectify the situation. The identity program developed by the firm for the six buildings of California Self Storage in Anaheim was largely determined by their prominent freeway exposure. The idea, explain the designers, was to project an image of "a friendly,

clean, and efficient self-storage facility to the passing motorist."

The *Casebook* jurors agreed that the use of bright colors and the scale of the oversize graphics do exactly that. Aside from being friendly and efficient, the graphics are recognizable, vibrant, crisp, with an industrial feel to them. "There's a functional quality to this that makes sense," said one juror.

The overall program, which included logotype, architectural details, graphics, color, and interior and exterior building

1. A towering identification sign ensures freeway readability.
2,3. Oversize lettering for building identification and directional signs conveys a crisp, functional quality.

2.

3.

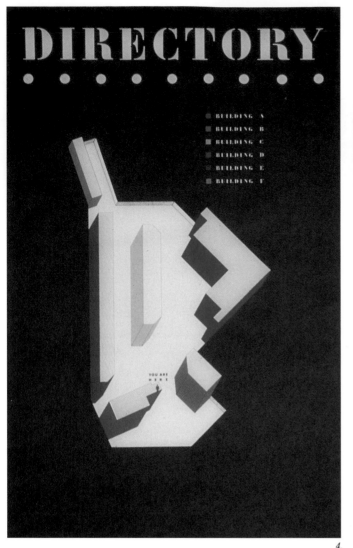

4.

4-7. *Storage facilities are coded by color and letter, making for an easily recognized identification system.*

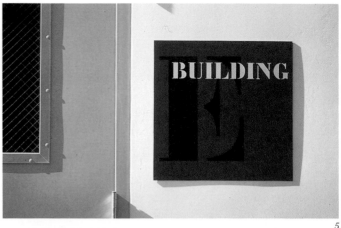

5.

6.

7.

finishes was based on the use of simple form and color with supporting graphics. A color code, comprised of six colors—green, lavender, yellow, blue, red, and orange—along with black-and-white, was developed to identify the individual buildings. Basic building materials—concrete, stucco, aluminum, etc.—conveyed an industrial feeling, as did the simple, unembellished logotypes selected—Corbu Stencil and Futura Medium.

The designers worked within a restricted budget and completed the identity program within the scheduled four months. Included in the schedule were extensive site studies investigating the facility's freeway exposure which were used to determine the placement of the graphics. This, the jurors agreed, made for an identity package entirely appropriate for the automobile-dominated lifestyle conventionally associated with Southern California.

Client: LIC, Inc., Los Angeles
Design firm: Sussman/Prejza & Co., Inc., Santa Monica, CA
Designers: Deborah Sussman, Scott Cuyler, Stephen Silvestri, Fernando Vasquez
Architect: Beck Moffett Associates
Fabricators: Coast Sign Display; Gene Siegrist Studio

Princeton Marketfair

A new generation of U.S. shopping malls can be distinguished by single-level arcades and by the absence of a major, large department store. Another quality that characterizes these newer malls is a greater effort to reflect regional interests and values. Such, at least, has been the case at Princeton Marketfair in New Jersey, whose designers have drawn inspiration from the rich folk-art traditions of the Delaware and Hudson valleys. Indeed, the tent kiosks, flags, wind vanes, and colorful wares sold from pushcarts all reflect the crafts and folk art indigenous to the area.

"The contemporary interpretation of folk-art themes befits the sophisticated atmosphere of the center," notes Phillips Engelke, the leader of the design team from Baltimore's RTKL Associates, in a reference to the affluent and educated Princeton market. Accordingly, the graphics program—including entrance structure and signing, retail kiosks, weathervanes, sculptures, flags, food-court signs, tenant signs, and movie marquees—celebrated the theme of a sophisticated country fair.

Working within an 18-month schedule and with a design

1. A free-floating aluminum ribbon edged in neon heralds the main entrance.
2-3. A folk-art theme is suggested by the logo.
4. A bright color palette for all signing is consistent with the festive country-fair theme.

1. 2. 3. 4.

5.

6.

7.

budget of $65,000, the designers first researched local folk-art traditions. Subsequently, they specified the use of cut, formed and routed aluminum plate for oversize sculptures—often 6′ to 8′ wide—that recall the form of antique weathervanes as well as cut and pressed tin folk art found in the region. Likewise, the use of cast iron suggests another local craft, and the design of gusset plates used in the trusswork is derived from quilt patterns. Finally, a lively color palette of reds, light blues, lavenders, golds, and light greens further contributes to the festive atmosphere.

Clearly, the Princeton Marketfair generates the sense of bustling commerce and excitement that is the objective of any shopping mall. More to the point, though, is its sensitivity to its region's native history and local crafts. It might, perhaps, serve as an example in an area of architecture and design that is dominated by a universal blandness.

Client: JMB Federated Realty, Cincinnati
Design firm/architect: RTKL Associates, Inc., Baltimore
Designers: Phillips Engelke, Striker Sessions, Allen Sears
Fabricators: Belsinger Sign Works
Lighting consultant: Theo Kondos Associates, Inc.

8.

10.

5-8. *A variety of sculptural elements constructed of cut aluminum plate are suggestive of antique weathervanes.*
9. *Cover of store design criteria booklet.*
10. *Checkerboard graphics evoking antique quilts embellish gusset plates in the trusswork.*
11. *Site plan.*

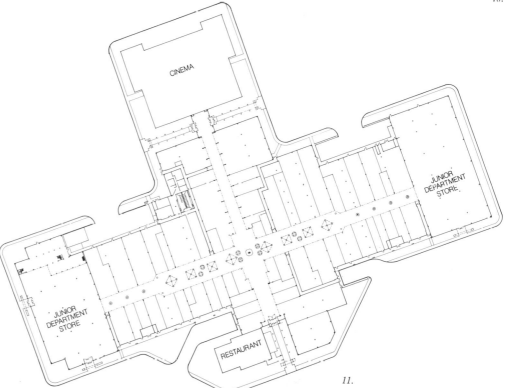

CINEMA

JUNIOR DEPARTMENT STORE

JUNIOR DEPARTMENT STORE

RESTAURANT

11.

The designers initiated the expansive graphics program for the upscale Owings Mills, Maryland, Mall by developing a distinctive logo that drew on local history. Discovering that Samuel Owings had been a leader in wheat production, operating a mill in the area in the 1700s, RTKL Associates of Baltimore created a stylized sheaf of wheat that appeared often in the design of site and food-court signing, mall directories, and other mall graphics. The wheat motif worked both as a logo and as a model for sculpture.

Over the main entrance, a sculptural element that translates the sheaf of wheat into three dimensions all but substitutes for conventional entrance signing. (Complementing the sculpture at the main entrance is a small, brass, back-lit entrance plaque at pedestrian height, an elegant example of graphic restraint.) The three-dimensional rendering of the logo was especially praised by the *Casebook* jurors. A combination of aluminum, fiberglass, paint, and gold leaf, the sculpture glimmers by day and night alike, playing with light somewhat as a real sheaf of wheat might.

As the designers explain, "We were trying to create an image of elegance to appeal to richer tastes." Painted metal, polished brass, and a white/ gold/green color palette were continued throughout the graphics program. Polished brass with pierced lettering and neon backing, for example, was used for entrance plaques; and for mall directories, a painted aluminum sculpture of sculpted wheat, bevelled glass, letters in

1.

gold leaf, and brass rails.

For the food-court Conservatory, signing was designed "to emphasize the light and airy and lacy and leafy quality of a conservatory." The entrance sign, then, was designed to evoke a garden lattice, stretching 30′ back into the food court. Gilt lettering

and sculpted branches of white "leaves"—constructed of painted sheet metal—and "flowers"—actually blue light bulbs—complete the garden idyll. Food-tenant banners within the Conservatory were constructed of aluminum panels with gold-ball spacers and screened graphics.

For retail-tenant signs elsewhere in the mall, back-painted plexiglass was specified, with aluminum brackets and brass logos. Together, these make for a consistent signing system that can nevertheless accommodate an elegant diversity.

The designers completed the

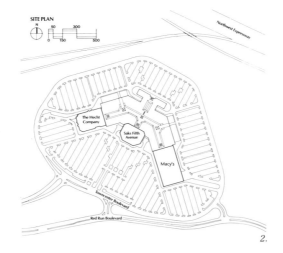

2.

OWINGS MILLS

3.

1. When translated into three dimensions, the stylized sheaf of wheat motif works as a sculptural element.
2. Site plan of upper level.
3. The wheat motif used as part of the logotype has a stencilled folk-art quality.
4. Wheat motif sculpture glitters during evening hours.

5.

6.

7.

signing program for the mall within the allotted nine-month time frame. Color samples and lighting variations were studied in mock-ups, and scale models were created to ascertain the design and placement of the sheaf-of-wheat sculptures and the Conservatory sign. In fact, says designer Ann Dudrow, "Without the models we never would have gotten the results we were looking for. They were less studies and more guides for fabrication." Indeed, it was these scale models that permitted graphic elements to become sculptural—the linear to be successfully translated to three dimensions. And they are the transformations that permit the environmental graphics of the Owings Mills Mall to achieve a stronger, more effective, and more final presence.

Client: The Rouse Co., Columbia, MD
Design firm/architect: RTKL Associates, Inc., Baltimore
Designers: Ann Dudrow, Andrea Cohen
Fabricators: Belsinger Sign Works

8.

9.

The Esplanade

1. *The graphic fan panel used at the entrance suggests the stained glass ornamentation that is nearly indigenous to the New Orleans area.*

1. *The graphic fan panel used at the entrance suggests the stained glass ornamentation that is nearly indigenous to the New Orleans area.*

1.

The Esplanade, located not far from New Orleans, stands out in the new genre of retail shopping malls that are designed to reflect the culture or history of their locale. As its designers explain, they have made an effort to "create the flavor of New Orleans without trying to duplicate the French Quarter." Even the name of the mall is a direct reference to an historic New Orleans street of the same name known for its prosperous residents and flamboyant, elegant architecture.

The first two-level shopping center in the New Orleans region, The Esplanade encompasses 1,446,500 square feet. Its focus is a centrally located, 20,000-square-foot food court with a series of stepped dining terraces. The program for architectural graphics included a project logo, entrance and site signing, fanlight graphic panels installed along the entire length of the promenade and food court, food court graphics, and coffee kiosk

By drawing on photographs of, and books about, the history and architecture of New Orleans, and by researching the area's folk traditions, the designers developed a visual program that made numerous specific regional allusions. Which, explains designer Phillips Engelke, was not difficult: "You don't have to reach very far to find New Orleans tradition. You practically fall over it."

As a central theme, then, the designers installed a series of fanlight graphic panels, 6' wide, constructed of painted aluminum, and lit with neon, running the length of the

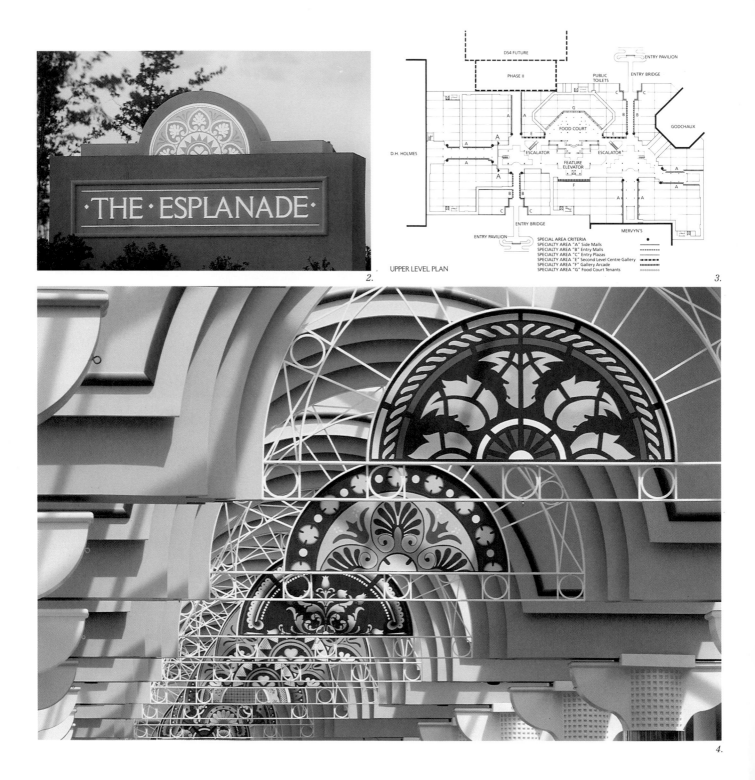

THE · ESPLANADE ·

UPPER LEVEL PLAN

2.

DS4 FUTURE

PHASE II

PUBLIC TOILETS

ENTRY PAVILION

ENTRY BRIDGE

D.H. HOLMES

G

FOOD COURT

GODCHAUX

ESCALATOR

ESCALATOR

FEATURE ELEVATOR

F

ENTRY PAVILION

ENTRY BRIDGE

MERVYN'S

SPECIAL AREA CRITERIA
SPECIALTY AREA "A" Side Malls
SPECIALTY AREA "B" Entry Malls
SPECIALTY AREA "C" Entry Plazas
SPECIALTY AREA "E" Second Level Centre Gallery
SPECIALTY AREA "F" Gallery Arcade
SPECIALTY AREA "G" Food Court Tenants

3.

4.

2. *Della Robbia typeface and a fan panel are used for entrance signage.*
3. *Site plan of upper level.*
4. *The series of fanlight graphic panels with lacy iron work creates a sense of color and festivity appropriate to the region.*
5. *Neon frames highlight a series of panels.*

5.

6.

promenade to suggest the radiant stained-glass windows indigenous to much of the city's architecture. Lacy ironwork surrounding the panels evokes the ornamental grillwork found elsewhere in the city.

The food court was designed with the French Market in mind—an outdoor columned arcade accommodating a farmers' market that offers an abundance of colorful, regional foods. The designers tried to reproduce the historic market's sense of abundance, as well as its sense of light. Explains Engelke, "We wanted the sun coming in, spilling over open patio spaces and terraces as it does in the French Quarter." Overall, the atmosphere of vibrant color and festivity evokes the excitement of Mardi Gras floats and costumes, an atmosphere of celebration, though without, as Engelke notes, "the seedy decadence." Architectural graphics were designed within a $45,000 design budget and one-year schedule. The *Casebook* jurors concurred that the imagery of The Esplanade graphics accurately and imaginatively projected its sense of place.

Client: Cadillac Fairview, White Plains, NY
Design firm/architect: RTKL Associates, Inc., Baltimore
Designers: Phillips Engelke, Linda McCloud, Ann Dudrow
Fabricator: Louisiana Sign Systems
Lighting consultant: Theo Kondos Associates, Inc.

7.

6, 7. Tenant signing in the food court conveys a sense of hearty abundance akin to that of the historic French market.